GREAT WESTERN
APPRENTICE

To the memory of my dear Parents

and to those thousands of nameless workers who,

over the years, with their labours,

fortitude and expertise made

Swindon Works renowned

and the name of the Great Western

into a near legend

GREAT WESTERN APPRENTICE

Swindon in the 'thirties

Hugh Freebury

Trowbridge

Wiltshire County Council

Library & Museum Service

1985

Published by Wiltshire County Council Library & Museum Service
Bythesea Road, Trowbridge, Wiltshire
Designed by Edward J. Kelly
Cover illustration by Kenneth Wood
Typeset by PCS Typesetting, Frome
Printed and bound by Bath Midway Litho Ltd, Bath
© as to text H. A. H. J. Freebury, 1985
© as to photographs (except First aid competition) British Rail/Railprint, 1985
ISBN 0 86080 137 3

Wiltshire County Council
Library & Museum Service

Contents

Acknowledgements

The publication of this book has been made possible by the enlightened policy of Wiltshire Library & Museum Service in publishing material relating to the county. I therefore wish to express my gratitude to its Director, Mr. R. L. Pybus, and the members of its staff who have been to such pains to ensure that my text should be made available to the public.

All the photographs used in the book, with the exception of that of the first aid competition, are reproduced by kind permission of British Rail/Railprint.

Illustrations

Introduction

So much has already been written about the Great Western Railway in general and its Swindon Works in particular, a further book on the subject may seem superfluous.

But this is a true factual account of what day-to-day life in the Factory was really like in the '30s, as seen through the eyes of an apprentice to one of the lesser trades. It is not an attempt to rob an era of its glamour, but rather to keep things more in perspective and show the forbearance and reactions of the workers in difficult times, and the effect the industry had on family life.

My remaining contemporaries, who worked with me in the famous A Shop during those years of significant developments, will know this is an honest endeavour to set things down frankly as we saw them and not, I hope, in a sense of bitterness or rancour.

I just wish the facts to speak for themselves.

H.F.

Into the working world

1

Monday was fast approaching, that first Monday of June 1932 awaited over the months with such mixed feelings. The previous week there had been a brief medical examination in the gaunt Park House on the corner of the G.W.R. estate at Church Place, then my father was told to make sure I reported to the Managers' Office in the middle of the Locomotive Works at 8.30 a.m.; and in respectable clothes! That was a considerable relief, for it meant I would start as an office boy somewhere in the huge complex of workshops sprawled on either side of the main railway line linking London and Bristol.

Actually I'd left school the previous Christmas, but since the 'Company', as it was commonly known in Swindon, would accept no school leavers before they were 14 years and 8 months, it meant either a return to school or finding some temporary stop-gap job to fill in the time meanwhile.

Much as I'd enjoyed those last few years at school, like most youngsters of the day I was anxious to get out into the world and have a shilling or so to rattle in my pocket. I sometimes made this point to one of my favourite teachers at the Elementary School I attended, but the retort of Mr. Veness always came back: "Yes, but don't forget you must go out for long hours to earn them first!"

We all knew that of course! But once school was really behind us it took only a couple of weeks for the novelty to wear thin and the reality to be brought home that there was no turning back, and it was up before 7 o'clock of a morning, six days a week.

I had taken my basic education most casually at the unprepossessing single floor school near the end of the long Rodbourne Road until I was ten. Then one morning in prayers the Head Teacher was ranting on about too many children making too little effort, while one unheeding pupil was passing a finger each side of the shiny brass button on his blue blazer and allowing his imagination to drift far away. Although the children   11

Setting out: the annual Trip, July 1934

stood close together, boys on one side girls on the other, the fuming Mr. Stevenson caught sight of my romancing and ordered me out before the whole school.

"Here is the very case in point!" he raged, so ferociously I was expecting to be cuffed any second. "This stupid boy Freebury is wasting his time even as I'm speaking!" he went on. "No wonder he makes no progress! He should be utterly ashamed of himself! He's got plenty of ability but is just too lazy to use it! Like many more of you he'd rather idle his time. If he wanted, and made up his mind, this boy could be top of his class!"

Such abject humiliation was bad enough, but my sister Jane was also there and the message would be going home with a meticulous certainty. But did 'Steevy', as we called him, really mean all this? Did I, Hugh Freebury, have more about myself than I was prepared to admit? Could I possibly be capable of working harder and reaching some achievement as my Headmaster implied? After suffering a light admonition from my mother, of whom I was very proud—and she of me I knew—I pondered over his words for many a day.

Not long after this incident I failed the Scholarship Examination, but being one of the youngest candidates was allowed a second try the following year and gained a so-called Free Place. This only really meant my parents wouldn't have to pay for my entry into higher education, as some better-off parents did whose children had failed; but everything else must be provided by the home—uniform, books, equipment and so on, all compulsory, as well as travel.

Now my father Harry Freebury, a pleasant, easy-going character, proud of my attractive though careworn mother and his three children, was only a second grade machineman 'Inside', and I knew my dedicated mother, shouldering as she did almost all family responsibility including budgeting, couldn't possibly afford to pay out for my education and keep us all reasonably clothed and fed. Indeed it was an unending struggle to achieve this even as things were.

Yet my mother asked me how I felt about this opportunity for a better education and if I decided on it they would find a way round the problem somehow. Knowing that if I had said "Yes" she would have worked herself still more to the bone, for she was already taking in two extra lots of washing to make ends meet, I unhesitatingly turned down the opportunity which might well have transformed my whole future. This was followed by a strong appeal from the educational authorities for my parents to reconsider the position, but I was firmly convinced it would all mean further deprivation and hardship for the rest of the family and stood by my original decision.

But those stinging words of Steevy rang again and again in my ears, and I gradually resolved to put them to the test. Without a word even to my mother I decided that by the time I reached the last class, Standard 7, I would leave as top pupil of the whole Elementary School. In due course I achieved this ambition quite comfortably before I was 14, and even gained the rare privilege of being Mr. Stevenson's personal monitor!

The geography teacher, that same Mr. Veness, took a real interest in all the keenest lads and encouraged us to think well ahead about the future. Those who wanted to go in the 'Factory', yet another common term for the railway works, he passed over gracefully since he could claim no influence in that direction, but went to great pains with the others to ascertain what they were interested in doing, and then endeavoured to get them fixed up with jobs around the town. He was a Careers Master well before his time, doing it purely out of concern for those he thought merited the effort; a truly kind and sincere man.

When I told him I was settling for the Factory, disappointment spread across the angular face, for he was far from handsome, yet a refreshing teacher for those rigorous times, devoting numerous out-of-school hours to other activities too, solely for his pupils' benefit. Even though he clearly disagreed with my decision, he made no attempt to persuade me to change my mind.

So my father went off to the Managers' Office, the block held in such awe by the workmen not only because of the four Works Managers there but also the numerous distinctive gentlemen clerks who held such sway, to see what trade they would offer his only son. One of these very reserved individuals looked up my father's status and finally decided they could accept me as an apprentice to boilermaking. This particular trade was considered one of the lowest and most commonplace of all, and my father produced my leaving Report. Could they not offer him on my 13 behalf at least the apprenticeship of a machineman like himself?

"No," was the emphatic reply. "You are only on the 40 shilling rate. If you were on the top grade we might consider it. Sorry."

So that two extra shillings a week made all the difference! They weren't in the least sorry of course. There was lots more young factory labour available in the town and surrounding villages because the G.W.R. had an almost virtual monopoly in the Borough. In fact Swindon was more of a complete railway town than any other in the country since the complete rolling stock, locomotives, carriages and wagons were all built and repaired there.

It must be said that the people who enforced these rules so inflexibly in those days looked upon themselves almost as an elite—the 9 o'clock staff. They dressed impeccably, walked around proudly and often spoke with a pretension implying the whole factory depended upon them, and the manual workers therefore of little consequence to its smooth running and efficiency. True, only a select few at one section of the offices, No. 8, wielded this absolute control over the destinies of the sons of all employees with such commanding authority.

Therefore I found myself earmarked for the mediocre apprenticeship to boilermaking—which many scoffed was "more of a disease than a trade". My mother was annoyed by this outcome because she felt her husband should have stood his ground and insisted on something better; and perhaps my father tacitly acknowledged this when he apologised to me and showed such unease whenever the subject was subsequently mentioned.

Meanwhile since the Company refused to take on youths immediately they left school, what should I do in those outstanding months? I could go back to school, though such a thing was far from fashionable and there was little more scope there anyway, so the obvious thing was a stop-gap job until the call came to join the masses who trundled the streets twice a day to be swallowed by the great conglomeration of workshops which dominated New Swindon.

Following a family consultation my father made the tedious journey up to the high Kingshill Bakery and with some relief found they were willing to take me on as a baker's boy, in reality

14   a roundsman's assistant, and learned I would be earning five

shillings a week for the first month and, if satisfactory, seven shillings and sixpence from then on, plus a small proportion of the commission earned on the sale of cakes and confectionery, which were also carried.

The words of Mr. Veness came back all too readily to me. There was quite an early morning trudge between the grim factory walls, under the even more depressing Rodbourne Bridges, down Park Lane and across Westcott Place to the filled-in canal, then up the long flight of formidable steps before the bakery was reached; and this in the depths of winter! The horse-van had to be loaded, old Tom harnessed and it was away by 8 a.m. After the first week it grew monotonous and tiring, there being no set time for knocking off since the round must always be completed; and once home at last there was the dispiriting thought of only a few hours to relax before considering bed in order to be up in time to start the round all over again! And Saturdays were worst of all.

Charlie Wright, my very first workmate, was a lively cheerful character who dearly loved a gossip, and each morning after we'd been going no more than an hour would call on his old mother who lived humbly behind the shops in the centre of the town and stay with her for anything up to half an hour. At least the kind soul would appear without fail holding a steaming cup of cocoa and call down the passageway: "Hughie, somethin' to warm the cockles of yer 'eart!"

I would much rather have got on with the round and finished earlier, but that was not the only stop for prolonged chit-chat on the way. Once, Charlie left the newly-painted van in a side street to disappear for another twenty minutes and I got so fed up with carrying the heavy bread basket to and fro, I decided to lead the horse and van into the main road. Unfortunately I didn't allow for the projecting arm of a street lamppost right on the corner which struck the candle lamp on the nearside of the van, splintering its glass with a crash and terrifying the horse, which promptly bolted with me clinging helplessly to the reins. There was an even more frightening crash when the wheels of the van collided with a window-cleaner's hand cart at the roadside, the horse leaping in terror and now hastening its flight, being eventually brought to a standstill by the timely intervention of a hefty bystander.

When he appeared and realised what had happened Charlie was on the verge of losing his temper until he appreciated my state of shock and distress, and after a further inspection of the van merely remarked: "Well, I don't exactly know what the foreman will say when he sees this tomorrow morning, but it cost a pretty penny to have this cart done up only a fortnight ago".

I hadn't the courage to tell my parents all that evening and suffered a particularly restless night before the confrontation took place. But the pallid, serious master-baker proved to be more conciliatory than I'd feared, emphasised I must never take charge of the horse again, and that some of my commission would have to be docked in due course to contribute towards the cost of repairing the damage.

So in that respect I was relieved when June came round and I could leave my first job after only a few months. Yet the prospect of having to serve a five year apprenticeship to boilermaking was even more daunting, for within myself I sincerely felt capable of better things. Still, there was a faint possibility that by the time I reached 16 another opening might come my way.

The Platelayers' Shop

2

When I was 11 I spent a long summer holiday with my favourite uncle and aunt in the sleepy village of Hambrook a few miles out of Bristol. My uncle was a shunter in the Stoke Gifford marshalling yard, and one day asked me if I wanted to make my way the two or three miles to the yard and watch the shunting, after his '2 to 10 turn' began. I arrived about 3o'clock that afternoon and settled on the high bank to watch the bustling tank engines nudging the trucks and wagons to and fro with such an interminable clatter, occasionally waving to my uncle as I espied him. After some time he beckoned me down to the sidings.

"How would you like a ride on the footplate?" he asked me. I was almost too overcome to reply, and was led to the steps of the 2700 pannier tank and helped up to meet the driver and fireman.

"Don't get in the way," my uncle cautioned me. And to Bill the driver: "When you get tired of him give me the nod."

I was so thrilled with this unexpected privilege I did my best to be inconspicuous yet watched every move of both enginemen until the time came for a break, when I was taken to the shunters' hut where I shared my uncle's tea and sandwiches. Operations were resumed after a lengthy period, and as dusk crept in towards the end of the shift the driver asked me to start the locomotive. I immediately went to the regulator and did my best to lift the handle but only with difficulty, yet the powerful little 0-6-0 snorted away until I was ordered to slow it down and jerkily applied the much shorter lever. It was a fitting climax to a wonderful day, implanting in my schoolboy heart a resolve to become a footplateman at all costs, years before the prospect of boilermaking raised its inauspicious head.

So, on that fresh Monday morning in June, there was still hope for me when about eight expectant office boys stood packed in the small ante-room of the Managers' Office waiting to be detailed to their respective posts. We all knew there were two 'post boys' required to work from the central office, one going east covering the smaller workshops and one westward in the direction of the massive A Shop. These two boys had to make the rounds delivering correspondence three or four times a day with a huge canvas post bag over one shoulder, but this had no appeal for me. My dearest hope was to be sent to the A Erecting Shop, the 'AE', where all the largest locomotives were repaired and where, in the farthermost corner, .the new work was carried out; in fact I'd almost made up my mind this was to be my posting. Alas, when some other name was called, a tall thin lad stepped forward and the resident office boy was directed to escort him to the AE.

I had learnt from my father the names and locations of most workshops and the kind of work each carried out. There was the X Shop, where a near neighbour was a chargehand, that machined all the rails and crossings, the L2 or Tank Shop where another neighbour was a chargehand, the Boiler Shop, the Q Shop where the blacksmiths operated, the P1 where the boilers were tested; and of course the A Shop complex, A Machine (AM) where my father worked, the A Boiler Bay (AV), and the A Wheel Shop (AW).

In addition all of us about to start in the Factory knew already of the notorious Bolt Shop, strangely enough almost adjacent to the Managers' Office, for it consisted of numerous small, raging furnaces for heating steel rods and alongside each of these a foot-operated press into which the white hot ends of the rods were thrust to emerge the other side as dull red bolts or nuts, merely requiring to be screwed or threaded. The dark murkiness of the shop, the roaring of the furnaces, the choking fumes which blackened the dingy windows and poured out of the doorway were reminiscent of a hell on earth. Every young lad dreaded being assigned there, and how relieved I'd been to learn that a clean appearance was required of me rather than working clothes!

One by one the other prospective office boys were singled off until at last my name was called by the porter. "Take this one to the Platelayers' Shop."

Platelayers' Shop? It was one I'd never heard of! Where on earth could it be? I was escorted past the B Shed where the smaller locos were repaired, along the end of the imposing C.M.E.'s Offices where those favoured elite carried out their duties and Mr. C. B. Collett himself controlled affairs, under a long subway beneath what is known as the Gloucester Branch, up the other side, then past the General Stores until we approached a long narrow red-brick building standing on its own.

"This end is the D Shop or Carpenters' Shop," explained my guide, "and at the other end is where you're going, the PL Shop."

It proved to be the smallest workshop in the whole railway works and, crestfallen, I followed him up a short flight of wooden stairs, past what was obviously the foremen's office, then stepped into a tiny square room only large enough for a desk and one table, the so-called shop office itself. Behind the desk sat a small round-shouldered old man with a curved nose, who peered over the top of his brass-rimmed spectacles eyeing me for several embarrassing seconds.

"H'm!" he grunted. "So you're the new boy they've sent me. You'll be taking over from this one at the table, and he'll show you all you've got to do. Sit down over there now—I'm busy."

A Monday morning was indeed the busiest time of the week in the PL Shop office. It was mostly an outstation department with the majority of the men being sent out around the G.W. network on pipe laying, linking up the water towers strategically placed about the system to the water columns, those pivoted gushers alongside the line with hanging leather spouts like deflated elephant trunks, always ready to quench the demands of the ever thirsty locomotive boilers.

Usually the men returned home for the week-end and checked in at the shop on Monday for another travelling ticket or a new assignment, though most preferred working week-ends for the double time and extra lodging allowances, especially when they were able to rough it in one of the repair vans often sent to the site with their tools. The travel tickets had to be obtained from the Managers' Office, which often meant two or three journeys across there within a couple of hours so that the men could catch the 9 a.m. to Paddington, the 9.55 to Wales, or the 11.15 to the South West. All this I learned in a short time.

Further, all four foremen—more than the largest workshop of all, the AE, could boast of—also put in an appearance every Monday morning, three of them being on outstation duty. It took me a few Mondays to sort them out in my mind because often they were away inside the hour. Head Foreman Street struck me as a   19

Manorbier Castle, *March 1935*

true Victorian character, short, stocky and proud of a white handlebar moustache most conspicuous against his florid complexion. Second Foreman Jefferson was of slighter build, upright, severe, a man of few words; and Foreman Woolton, youngest by far of the three, was tall, thin and brown, spoke with a noticeable country accent and was obviously still finding his feet in his recently promoted position.

The fourth of these varied characters was Stanley Burton, another reminder of former times, short, podgy, again with a heavy moustache but this time one more of a russet hue; and he possessed twinkling eyes above rounded cheeks which suggested he could be quite human at times. He was the 'Home' Foreman and I was to see more of him than the rest put together. All these important individuals were immaculately turned out, Street and Burton in their navy blue, Jefferson in grey, while Woolton inevitably favoured thick tweeds. And of course, each sported that hallmark of foremen everywhere—the traditional bowler hat.

Don Baxter, the lad I was replacing, himself proved to be something of a character. He had a broad unsmiling face with a hare-lip which unfortunately helped to make him appear quite cynical. But his was a devil-may-care attitude, and he soon made it clear he could hardly wait to embark on his apprenticeship as a fitter, turner and erector, most coveted and prestigious of all the trades in the railway works.

When I was settled in he gave me a nudge and nodded in the direction of the preoccupied clerk, who was in the process of rebuking someone at the head of the queue outside the pigeon-hole window. "His name's Sidney—Sidney Fox. A bit crotchety, but then he's knocking on. Too old for it really, the job I mean. But too old for that as well, I reckon. He's not so bad as long as you do just what he wants."

Poor Sidney was certainly being harassed. Apart from the restive line-up outside the small sliding window, first one of the outstation foremen then another would come through the intervening door of their office with a piece of paper and/or a further request, and while the clerk was always deferential towards them his temper grew more frayed with the persistent line of workers peering through the glass; with never a moment to clear the glistening dew-drop that resided almost permanently at the end of his sharp round nose. Presently he turned to us, still sitting at the table, and spoke to Don Baxter. "Take him to the Managers' Office, son. I must have these tickets at once."

As soon as we were clear of the small workshop Don said: "Phew! I shall be bloody glad to get out of that place. Always like that on a Monday morning—nothing but murder! Mind you, the rest of the week's not so bad. Tell you what, p'raps even better than in a big office, even if the time sometimes drags. Better get a move on!"

Towards the end of the first day he took me to the far end of the workshop which was partitioned off into a separate department specialising in fire-hose fittings and other fire-fighting fitments. Three men were working at benches and he went up to the first one. "Hello Pinhead," he greeted the man. "Any luck last night?"

Pinhead looked about 50, had a neatly trimmed moustache over fairly thick lips, and as he turned, still filing at the brass ferrule in the vice, there was a mischievous look in his alert eyes. "No, Warn't up to it. Can't keep it up like you young 'uns, you know. How about you?"

"Nothing doing, no chance. It's me night school night. Starting in the R Shop next week. This is the new office boy."

Pinhead acknowledged me with a nod and knowing wink, then we left him. It was only when we dropped in on him periodically over the next couple of days with similar exchanges taking place that I realised what they alluded to. Although boys referred vaguely to the facts of life at school, I was not quite prepared for such frequent references to these things, but soon found myself having to accept it as part of the earthiness and monotony of the manual worker's daily existence, though I felt no desire to participate in such banter myself.

On the second day, coming away from the customary visit to the Managers' Office, Don Baxter poked me in the back. "Come on, I'll show you round a bit." We went through a wide open doorway into a remarkably quiet workshop. "This is the G Shop. They're millwrights here; all skilled fitters. You'll come here because apart from working on these turntables they assemble the water columns—you know, those things that fill the tenders with water."

I learned later this was the original Boiler Shop built with its arched walls nearly 100 years ago. I saw the shop office high against one wall, then was told: "Now we'll go through the Spring Shop!"

What a contrast! Here was bustle and noise and in particular the constant ringing of hammers on anvils, for there were several forges at full blast and out would come a strip of dazzling hot metal to be knocked into shape as a leaf for a multiple spring. There were also machines for rolling white-hot, round bar into coil springs, which were then thrown down and left to cool. No one appeared to be idle and though the clangour, bustle and ceaseless activity were almost frightening, I was fascinated and could have lingered longer.

"Had enough?" called my companion above the reverberating din. "Better get back or Sidney'll wonder what we've bin up to!"

I followed him out of the other end of the Shop to be confronted by several sidings, which we immediately began to cross.

"Follow me!" said my guide. "We're going to cross the main line!"

I instantly drew back. I'd heard enough about the railway works already to know this was a strictly forbidden procedure.

"No, that's wrong!" I protested. "Nobody is allowed to do that. I'm not coming."

"Don't be chicken!" Don Baxter taunted me. "I do it lots of times. Come on, follow me! Or you'll get left behind!"

I was in a dreadful dilemma. I wanted to stay in his favour since he'd been very helpful so far, but I had an urgent burning fear of getting caught and what the consequences would be. Back over the years whenever a man was apprehended doing this by the watchmen—you never knew who they were because they wore no uniform, being deliberately nondescript—a ruthless example was made of him by instant dismissal, news which spread around the Factory and the whole town within hours.

My heart thumping at a frightening pace, I started out crossing further rails one by one, obscured at first by standing wagons, in itself most dangerous. Then we reached the Gloucester Branch, but really the main line to that city forking out from Swindon Station and entitling it to the distinction of 'Junction'.

24   There they were! The four highly-polished rails curving round

sharply one way up to the station, but presenting an unobstructed view in the other direction. We two miscreants looked at each other wordlessly for a couple of seconds then Don made a dash for it with me in hot pursuit; but not before I'd caught sight of the signalman in the Rodbourne Lane signal box some 80 yards away. I was certain we'd been seen and would be reported, but it was now too late to turn back and there were still more sidings to cross on the opposite side. I eventually reached the comparative safety of the far roadway trembling all over more from fright than the exertion.

"What's the matter mate?" my laughing colleague teased me. "Didn't you get a thrill out of that? It's a bloody terrific challenge!"

"If you want to do it again," I replied quite breathlessly, "you do it on your own. I'm always going round the long way."

"Well, that's saved a bit of time anyway," he retorted. "Now we can see what's doing down the Running Shed."

Running Shed? I could hardly believe my ears. "Did you say the Running Shed? Where is it? Is it very far?"

"Course not stupid! That's it down there right in front of you. Can't you see the engines?"

It was absolutely incredible. Here was the one place I hoped to be when I was 16, immediately opposite the PL Shop and less than a stone's throw away! Now I felt, by deliberately placing me so near my heart's desire, Fate had been kind to me after all; in fact I couldn't have been any closer, and just stood there surveying the place of my dreams for the first time.

Outside the dim, smoky interior stood three impressive giants which I would soon be able to identify at a glance. There was a *Saint*, known by everyone in the works as a '29', putting on a pleasing appearance though showing her years in dullish paintwork; a *Star*, commonly known as a '40', in a somewhat similar faded condition; but then nearest to me was an immaculate *Castle*, her bodywork proud in its fresh green coat, brasswork agleam about her smoke stack, around her safety valve and those same touches to her cab and splashers. She it was that riveted my attention and made me more resolved than ever that one day I would command her or one of her sisters! As I continued to stare her driver completed his oiling, slowly mounted the wide 25 steel footsteps to the cab and disappeared from view. No. 5006 *Tregenna Castle*. What a lovely name! Little did I know that a few months later she would be making a record-breaking run on the *Cheltenham Flyer* at an average speed of 81.7 m.p.h. for the 77.3 miles to Paddington.

"Come on!" broke in my unappreciative companion. "What you staring at? You'll be sick of the sight of 'em before you're finished."

"Never!" I thought, keeping my ambition to myself as we walked on to the shop office. And nearer the time I would badger my father regularly about getting my name to the top of that Running Shed list of engine cleaners, until my call finally came.

26

Swindon skyline

Office routine and a sad ending

3

That first week with the retiring office boy going through the daily procedures went all too quickly. In common with all Swindon residents I had learned over the years to live with the factory hooter, its mournful drone swelling out and echoing across the town and countryside several times a day. It was said, when the weather was appropriate, it could be heard as far as Wootton Bassett to the west and beyond Shrivenham to the east. It warned employees and others it was time to rouse themselves from sleep almost an hour before checking-in time, then blared again at ten minutes to eight, gave a short blast at five-to, then the long final warning that time was up at 8 o'clock. Down promptly came the glass windows of all check boxes in the factory, and anyone even a few seconds too late must now be signed in by the foreman, who often required an explanation for the lapse, and "lose a quarter" as a consequence.

For the mid-day break the hooter broke out again at 12.30, cautioned everyone they should be on their way back at 1.20, gave a short intermediate blast at 1.25, then the long decisive bellow at 1.30. The hooter signalling the end of the normal working day seemed nothing like so doom-laden, and was accepted with relief by most people both inside the Works and outside, at 5.30 p.m.

To me the deep-throated summons to work now took on a personal significance and I resolved to be a good time-keeper and never lose a single 'quarter'. To this end I soon realised I could use what was called the "Gas Works Entrance" to get home more quickly, so-called because the Company's own considerable gas works—the largest private gas-producing plant in the country— was situated there at the extreme northern edge of the sprawling railway complex. I must always check in on time, but was allowed to check out a few minutes before the hooter provided the Foreman had left, though as Foreman Burton also used the same exit I must be sure I was well in the rear until that worthy gentleman had mounted his sturdy green cycle by means of its 27 back-step and pedalled off down the long straight lane leading into the main thoroughfare of Cheney Manor Road.

By taking a few short cuts along the backways of the streets for which the town is noted—as children we always called them "backsies"—then entering our home from the rear I found I could make it in under 10 minutes, which gave me 40 minutes at midday; ample time since I was rarely kept waiting for my meal by my loving, thoughtful mother. I now took a little pride in being the second bread-winner in the family, for my elder sister had been apprenticed to millinery in the largest store in the town at a mere pittance a week, which phenomenal sum she was allowed to keep in the hope of providing her own clothes. Since this meant she could neither afford a lunchtime snack nor even a bus fare, she walked the three miles return to 'business' twice a day. My younger sister would be at school for another three and a half years.

Now a keen office boy, I was firmly resolved to make a good impression in my new job and to that end made detailed notes of each day's routine so that when left to my own devices I would not be completely at a loss. On our daily journeys that first week we inevitably passed through the B Shed (though this didn't meet with official approval) and having seen one of the earliest prints of the Repair Shop I was certain this was the one. It consisted of a row of bays on either side of a lower traversing road along which rolled the traversing table, capable of drawing locomotives outside the Shop onto its own pair of rails by means of pulleys on bollards and transporting them inside to the engine pit awaiting them.

At this time the B Shed was utilised for repairs of only the smaller engines, 0-6-0 tanks—the 22s and 23s, the 4-4-0s—the 32s, 33s and 34s (*Dukes* and *Bulldogs*) and so on. I was soon quite interested in watching these being stripped down day by day and then take shape again gradually over the weeks or months, but was much more enthusiastic about the 4-6-0s which I rarely saw under repair since they were dealt with some half a mile westward in the extensive tall A Shop.

Attached to the B Shed was the R Shop, packed with busy machines of all types and sizes, while in one corner was the 'nut scragging' section where most aspiring fitters and turners began their apprenticeship threading the blank nuts and bolts spewed out by the impatient stamping presses of the Bolt Shop not far away. Don Baxter took me there a couple of times during my week of probation and spoke to the Chargeman to make sure he would be known the following Monday. The whirr and clatter of the machines, the sickening stench of the cooling oils and the monotonous rattle as the finished items dropped into the metal boxes turned me instantly against being a fitter and turner had I been given the chance, and I thought again of the escape from all this commotion when my time came to be an engine cleaner.

On the first Friday morning my mentor showed me an oval copper-coloured check in place of the usual brass one for timekeeping and explained it was used for the weekly pay.

"You ain't got one," he explained, "because you got the 'Grand March Past' today. You always get paid a week behind."

Around eleven o'clock that morning the Checkie set up a peculiar black table in the middle of the shop with a flat narrow top and sloping brass centre-piece. At paying-out time the workers lined up according to their check numbers and as each number was called out the oval check was placed down and one Pay Clerk slipped it into a container as his colleague slapped a little round tin bearing the man's number onto the table. Each man walked a few yards away, opened the tin, checked his money tallied with the pay-slip inside, replaced the lid and deposited it in the basket provided.

When on holiday as a schoolboy my pals and I would occasionally go up the Town to the Golden Lion Bridge and watch all the money to pay the employees being brought out from the bank on the corner. It was always carried out in blue bags and stacked in a peculiar four-wheeled, enclosed hand cart, with an extremely tall ex-guardsman type of individual supervising the operation closely. We all knew him to be the Head Watchman of the Works, and often speculated if he was really carrying a pistol on his person since his hands were inevitably thrust in the pockets of his jacket or long overcoat.

This cart was then manhandled to the Tunnel Entrance exactly opposite the Mechanics Institute, under the subway and up to the Pay Office, part of the C.M.E.'s block, where Wages Clerks were ready to break it down into wages and pack it in the little round 29 tins. All this was done each Friday morning and with 10,000 employees and more it was amazing how few mistakes were made.

The men had a good idea how much they'd earned the previous week because on the Wednesday morning I had to go to the Wages Office to collect the time-sheets for the workshop. That first week Don Baxter showed me how much some of the outstation men earned in overtime and lodging allowances, but if we had been caught perusing this private information we would have been in serious trouble. Since the Foremen and Clerks were on the Staff their sheets were not included, and we were left speculating how much they got.

I stayed behind for a short while the first week to watch the procedure of paying out, which was not allowed to commence till the Foreman was present; while another rule was once you'd left the Shop you had accepted that your pay and pay-slip agreed. Since the Platelayers' Shop got its name from the men who oiled and checked the points and crossings around the works there was quite a queue lined up behind the table yet it was surprising how quickly they were paid out.

I soon grew most content with my lot, a clean job, regular hours and, as previously hinted, duties that were not too exacting. Though I wasn't given any scope to prove my worth I did my best to please my conscientious but easily harassed superior who, from remarks passed here and there, was apparently within a few months of retirement. If I grew relieved when the Monday rush was all over, Sidney certainly did! He proved most vulnerable to remarks like: "Come on Sidney! We got a train to catch!"

"If thee talks like that," was the inevitable reply, "I shall turn a deaf ear on thee! The good Lord only gave I one pair of hands, same as thee."

Sidney hailed from the village of Chiseldon six miles away, and when incited was inclined to forget his singular position and drop back into his country brogue. Some of the men took pleasure in rattling him in this way, for peering poker-faced over those thin-rimmed spectacles perched half way down his arched nose with its attendant dew-drop perhaps he did remind them of some cartoon character. His face rarely gave even the hint of a smile, yet it was said he had a crippled wife to whom he was devoted, and if he was handled the right way he could be reasonably pleasant.

When I was thoroughly into the routine of the work I was able to study more closely the responsibilities of Sidney and how he coped with them, so that by the time he approached retirement I felt almost capable of taking the seat at his desk. When his successor came to take over it was evident things were going to be different in the office. Thin and almost frail, the new Clerk was much younger and though he almost ignored me until Sidney had departed, I was sure we would get on well.

Mr. Hilton, a former Shop Clerk who had been temporarily transferred to the 9 o'clock Staff in the Managers' Office after a serious illness and major operations, was now deemed fit to return to his proper place on the 8 o'clock Staff if only to emphasise the inviolable difference between the two grades, and he was fully aware of this. But he had no previous experience of dealing with the mass of outstation work the PL Shop undertook and within days was asking me how Mr. Fox dealt with this and handled that; as I guided him he seemed to warm to me.

He was on a strict non-fat diet because of his stomach disorder and drank goat's milk regularly from a flask; but it didn't prevent him enjoying a gossip, and, relying on me more and more, would leave the office for some while, making the acquaintance of all about him. It was something I grew to relish, for I became more confident in handling the phone and replying to people of consequence including the Assistant Manager with whom the workshop was most closely connected.

One morning a message came through which shocked Mr. Hilton so that he rushed into the Foreman's office leaving the door ajar.

"Mr. Burton," he announced, "I've just had the news that the Old Man has been killed!"

"The Old Man?" queried the Home Foreman, tilting his bowler towards the back of his head and raising his prominent brows.

"Yes. Oh I'm sorry. Mr. Churchward, Mr. G. J. Churchward."

"Good heavens, no! When? How come?"

"Apparently this morning about half past ten. On the line, not far from his house. I believe they said it was the Fishguard express."

At the time it meant but little to me other than the tragedy of 31 a violent death and the fact that he was the one who lived in the tall red house at the far end of Dean Street (named incidentally after his predecessor) and alongside the London to Bristol main line. Only in later years was I to learn what a major contribution Mr. Churchward made to locomotive development not only on the G.W.R. but internationally also. His sturdy, efficient and handsome designs had been standardised and among others were the *Saints* (29s) and *Stars* (40s) which I always stopped to admire. Indeed my favourite *Castles* and *Kings* were little more than extended modifications of that great man's pioneering designs.

I heard it all again from my father that evening, for the whole town was shocked. Many wondered how it could have come about since it was said that 'Churchward' as he was also affectionately called knew the time of every train that passed his house to the minute, and the rumour was started that his sight and hearing were failing and perhaps he had some notion of the consequences of leaning over the line on a murky morning. It was even suggested he had distributed his Xmas gifts to his servants well in advance for the very first time. But he had been warned about taking more care, and accidental death was the only possible verdict in the circumstances. Any of the thousands of employees who wished were given paid time off to pay homage to the Chief Mechanical Engineer who firmly established his railway as the most successful and reliable in the country, and the streets of Swindon were lined with clerks, artisans of every description and their mates who bared their heads in reverent silence as the cortège made its way to the Old Town Parish Churchyard high on Swindon Hill where the great Devon man was finally laid to rest.

In the course of time I learned more of the immense contribution George Jackson Churchward had made to locomotive design, particularly his firm emphasis on standardisation. In that direction, for instance, he soon established a piston of 30in. stroke inside a cylinder of 18in. diameter, combining this with a round (piston type) valve of 10½in. diameter, and was a believer in the greatest possible exhaust of steam. Equally important was his development of the locomotive boiler, something I was to learn much closer at hand in the years ahead.

In 1902 the great pioneer produced *William Dean,* No. 100, the first 4-6-0 locomotive of its kind to appear in Britain, so outstanding in design with outside cylinders and uncluttered appearance it had become accepted as the link between Victorian and modern locomotive development. The following year No. 98 had appeared, an improved all-Churchward 4-6-0 with partly tapered boiler and enlarged steam ports. She was later numbered 2998, a forerunner of the 2900 class I'd heard so much about from my father and others, noted for their efficiency and smooth running when the merits of the various Great Western 4-6-0s were being discussed.

In June of that same year, 1903, a heavy goods locomotive came onto the scene, a 2-8-0 numbered 97, and in the following September a 2-6-2 side tank No. 99 made its debut, prototypes of many more to follow in each class. Yet another type began to roll out of the workshops in 1904, the 4-4-0 *Cities,* of which perhaps the *City of Truro* became most famous. The following year another innovative No. 40 appeared, a 4-4-2 called *North Star,* the first four-cylinder locomotive to appear in this country; she was later modified to a 4-6-0 and became the forerunner of the renowned *Star* class.

Even so the creative genius of this brilliant man was still not exhausted, for in 1907 he designed and produced the first 4-6-2 Pacific engine to run on British rails. As a young schoolboy I well remember the *Great Bear,* as she was called, being so keenly talked about, since she was the pride of so many Swindon workers. But I was never lucky enough to see her because though effective in design No. 111 was not a great operating success, her unusual weight and size limiting her serviceability on the G.W. system; so later she was modified into a *Star* 400 class.

With the exception of this Pacific, the only one for many years on our railways, and the 3800 *County* class of 4-4-0s introduced in 1904 but known as "Rough Riders", I saw for myself how Churchward's designs were so fundamental, reliable and efficient they were not basically altered throughout the succeeding years of the famous Company he had served so competently. Even the popular *Castles* and *Kings* of his successor, Mr. C. B. Collett, were logical extensions of this great man's innovations, maintaining the same clean exterior and reliable functioning so

33

characteristic of all Great Western locomotives.

Gradually learning these things, I couldn't read enough about such an outstanding personality, and could easily picture him with his firm features, wide moustache and tweed suits resembling in appearance some country squire more than a brilliant engineer, enjoying a bachelor's life in his relaxing periods at the house down beyond the A Shop and on the other side of the main London to Bristol line; *Newburn House* it may be formally called, but to me and many other ordinary inhabitants of the district it would always be known as "Churchward's House". From there he usually walked along the side of the Works to his office, and it is said he might be sitting on a stool waiting for a draughtsman to appear for duty and continue with a problem discussed the day before, greeting him with words like: "Come along my boy. Time to get on with it".

When, later, I became associated with the first man on the scene of that tragic accident one misty December morning and heard a few more details less generally known, it was almost as if I was present at the untimely and ironic end of a famous person dispatched so abruptly by the very might of something he had helped to create.

Restless ambition

4

Over the months I never failed to stop and study the numerous locos making their way to and from the Running Shed or standing outside. I always hurried my journey to the Managers' Office so that I could spend five or ten minutes watching the routine of coaling, watering and oiling. I learnt to recognise at a glance all the familiar types and their class numbers. Once I saw the rare 3800 *County* class 4-4-0 with outside cylinders, no doubt soon to be consigned to the scrapyard. One class always confused me because they were everywhere, the 4300s, 53s and 63s, often called *Moguls*. Another confusing group was the 2-6-2Ts, numbered 3100, 4100 and 5100, along with the 45s and 55s.

One particular class I always watched for was the 2-8-0 47s, for they had a large boiler and bigger driving wheels than the slower 2-8-0 goods, the 2800s. It was a privilege to spot one, not just because only nine of the former were built by Churchward, but their duties were mostly on fast freight trains at night. I wondered if in due course I would be lucky enough to espy them all.

Sometimes I might go into the Running Shed, using the side access door immediately opposite the PL Shop. There, ranged around the huge turntable head-on, was a motley array of engines, large and medium, some dead and some in steam, an odd one gleaming but many looking dusty and neglected. On certain days of the week there would often be a 4-6-0 L.N.E.R. and I was intrigued by the comparable crudeness of its appearance alongside our beautiful *Castles* and *Kings*.

I was also fascinated by the skill of the drivers nudging one of the latter onto the turntable, for there was very little space to spare at the front end or behind the tender. Then began the slow process of manually turning the monster about itself in the direction required, a tremendous effort being needed to first get it moving. The engine always slid onto the turntable with a hefty thump and left it in the same way. Much as I disliked grease and dirt, the smell of hot oil somehow appealed to me and I knew I

Newburn House, Churchward's home

would be happy here polishing these engines and learning the names of all their various parts and how they worked, as quickly as possible, so that I could qualify as a light fireman.

When my sixteenth birthday grew nearer I became rather apprehensive in spite of the fact I would qualify for an increase of 2/6d a week. That unwelcome apprenticeship might yet become a reality.

I'd first persuaded my father I wanted to work in the Running Shed as soon as I'd left school and he decided to have a chat with a neighbour across the backs who was already a train driver of some experience, though it was not easy to catch him in because of the peculiar hours all drivers worked. One day he was lucky.

"What on earth do 'e want to take this job up for?" asked the driver, George Gorton, to my father's astonishment.

"Well, you know how it is with young lads . . ."

"Yes I do," put in George, "because they think it's all glamour. Believe me it's not." It wasn't exactly what my father had come to hear. "I suppose 'e knows 'e'll 'ave to start as a cleaner, and a pretty messy and boring job it is I assure you. Not only that, we got some of 'em going on for 20 and they're still at it!"

"Well he won't take 'No' for an answer so far," replied my father, "and I wondered how I go about getting his name down."

"H'm!" grunted the driver, as if disappointed his negative advice was having no effect. "You'll have to go to No. 19 Office in the C.M.E.'s and give 'is particulars. They'll tell you it's too early and there's a long waiting list, but try and push them to put 'is name down."

Father got permission from his Chargehand on the Planers' Gang in the AM Shop and went off to the imposing offices. He had no trouble finding No. 19 for it was on the ground floor and one of the first doors through the entrance of the long tall block. He knocked timidly and waited for the "Come in!"

Two smartly-dressed clerks looked up enquiringly from their desks but their looks darkened somewhat when they saw the shortish man in his middle forties wearing a soiled slop and patched overalls. Instinctively they sat back as if there were some fear of contamination.

"I've come to see if I can have my son's name put down for the Running Shed," explained my father.

"Oh," said one with sharp features and sleek dark hair. "Are you in the Works?"

"A machineman," nodded father. "In the AM."

The first one glanced across at his colleague, whose expression gave nothing away. He turned back to my father, weighing him up shrewdly.

"How old is he?"

"About fourteen and a half. But he's very keen, and bin like it ever since he was twelve and had a turn on the footplate of a shunting engine. Perhaps I didn't ought to say that," he added cautiously.

"No, quite so," was the cold reply. "Well I'm afraid he's too young yet, and must realise there's a very long waiting list and not many vacancies."

"I would still like his name to go down if you don't mind. I can't talk him out of it."

"He's still too young and will have to wait. Come back and see us when he's fifteen."

"But—but could you just put his name down so's I could tell him, please?"

"We'll see you again when he's fifteen," repeated the clerk frigidly, and my father realised the interview was over.

I was indignant when I heard all this and was determined not to let my father forget the matter. Promptly when I was 15 I worried my father to go there again, and though I knew he felt rather out of place in such austere surroundings he eventually returned to the offices and had my name duly entered at the bottom of the list. Neither was he allowed to let it rest there, for I pressurised him to have another word with Driver Gorton in the hope he might make some mention in the ear of the Shed Foreman. My Dad was lucky to catch the driver in the Working Men's Club in the next street when he made his weekly visit to pay into the Sick Fund.

"I've managed to get the lad's name down at last," said father, offering to buy the other a drink which fortunately he declined. "They wouldn't put him down on the list until he was fifteen."

"You mean the foolish lad's just as keen? I thought p'raps you'd manage to put 'im off."

"Never been set on anything like this before."

"Well, all I can say 'e wants to 'ave 'is 'ead read. I wouldn't let one of me own lads go on it, and you won't see many drivers as will. I expect 'e'd 'ave to start as a call boy."

"A call boy?"

"Ah. They're sent round in the early hours knocking us up. Otherwise 'alf on us wouldn't turn up for duty. That way we got no excuse. An' I'll tell you another thing . . ." And he went on so much my father began to wonder why he'd approached him in the first place, with doubts regarding my burning ambition really taking hold.

"If after all that," concluded Driver Gorton, "the lad is still not put off don't let them forget 'is name. Keep on going up there until they get tired of you and call 'im up. Every couple of months I'd say." I'm sure father was sorry he told me this because I made certain he never missed.

One day in the PL office Mr. Hilton asked me if I was related to Tim Freebury, a Chargehand on the shapers in the AM Shop, where he'd once worked in the Shop office. I said he was my grandfather and that my father also worked in the Shop as a machineman.

"Oh yes," he responded after a moment's hesitation. "On the planers I believe. I can place him now. What apprenticeship has your father got lined up for you?"

When I told him the Shop Clerk was appalled.

"What? Good heavens!" he retorted. "They're worth two a penny! You're deserving of something better than that, my son. Hasn't your father stuck out?"

"Well, they won't offer him anything better because he's only a second class machineman on 40/- a week. If he was on 42/- I think he might have got me on a machine."

"And that's not good enough either. H'm! I'll have to give it some thought and see what I can do."

It gave me a slight hope, especially when a few days later Mr. Hilton announced he would be away for some time and left me in charge for over an hour. He said nothing when he eventually arrived back, but at tea that evening my father said: "Mr. Hilton's been down to see me about you. He asked me what I was doing letting you go to boilermaking. I told him I done all I could, but it was all they would offer me. He said what a great help you been

38

since he came and you were cut out for office work. He was going to see what he could do for you."

Could there really be such a chance for me? I would even be willing to forego my unswerving ambition to work on the footplate for the prestige of being the humblest of Shop Clerks! Apart from all other considerations, once taken on it was a permanent job, unlike that of manual workers who could be sacked whenever railway receipts were down and there must be cutbacks, about every two or three years.

A week or so later Mr. Hilton went off again, this time saying openly he would be across at the Managers' Office. Apart from the private offices of the Managers, that grim square building in the heart of the Factory comprised the Main Office controlling the general running of the Locomotive side, the Wages Office and the Cost Office. It was also the den of the Managers' Chief Secretary, by title head of all the clerks in the loco works, a tall, severe, well-built gentleman with large spectacles commonly referred to by his surname, Wellard, and held in great reverence by all who came into contact with him even, it was said, the somewhat deferential Head Manager.

I knew instinctively the purpose of Mr. Hilton's visit. And how each moment dragged waiting for his return and hoping that I would be brought fully into the picture. I was!

Mr. Hilton enquired if there were any problems while he was absent and I referred to my notes regarding messages.

"Good," he said, settling down in the chair I vacated as soon as he'd returned. "Now I want you to listen carefully to what I've got to say, son. I've been to see Mr. Wellard on your behalf and I'll be frank and tell you exactly what happened. I told him what a great help you'd been to me coming into the unusual work of this office and that I was certain you could run this job on your own. I put a number of your good points before him especially how trustworthy you are—but don't let it go to your head—and pointed out in my view you'd be completely wasted as a boilermaker, and should be given the opportunity of putting your talents to better use."

A wave of embarrassment swept over me, but I could hardly wait for the outcome.

"Mr. Wellard listened to all I had to say very carefully and then   39 said this: 'Tell the lad to go ahead with his apprenticeship. A note will be made of what you've reported and will be put down on his indentures. His progress will be watched.'"

Try as I may, I couldn't conceal my abject disappointment, and the clerk saw this. He had no children of his own, but the way he spoke of his wife I'm sure they were a loving couple.

"Yes, I know how you feel, and I'm very sorry lad. Believe me I couldn't have done more if you were my own boy. Do your best to accept it, and remember at least your name has been brought to notice."

Yes, there was that small crumb of comfort at the end, but I hadn't felt so crestfallen for many a day and could not get home quickly enough to give expression to my feelings. Around the tea table I gave my parents an accurate account of what had been said and my mother in particular listened carefully and proudly. While she loved all three of us I knew she leaned just that little more to her only son, and I tried to be all she could have wished, truthful, sincere and very concerned for her welfare.

"Never mind Hugh," she tried to console me, stretching out her hand. "You've done well and we're both proud of you. It was too much to expect. There's a lot of things wrong in this world and one of them is you got to have somebody, or know somebody, if you want to get on. There's an awful lot of jealousy about and snobbery too, and as you get older you'll find you've just got to live with it. But I'm not ashamed of any of my children or the way I've brought them up, and as long as we can manage to keep our heads above water I'll be satisfied and count my blessings. Finish off your tea now."

"Your mother's right Hugh," added my father. "Just have faith and it will all work out in the end."

So within a couple of weeks I had to train my successor into the duties of office-cum-errand boy.

"Try to be polite and help everybody," I told him, "and you should be all right for a Christmas box. Have a little book in your hand when you go round the shop, and don't forget the outstation men on a Monday morning. I did well from them last year, nearly £4 altogether."

This was a tradition all office boys tried to pass on and those in the large workshops usually did extremely well if they were liked. Even during the working week an office boy might pick up a small tip going to the Tunnel Entrance in work's time to obtain the cheap privilege rail tickets wanted by the men, though some foremen frowned on this and it must be done secretly.

I showed the new boy all the likely places he must know and would have to visit, including the Drawing Stores behind the R Shop. Here on wooden rolls with a brass tab nailed on the end for identification were wrapped hundreds of thousands of working drawings stored in racks two storeys high, with details of every locomotive on the G.W. system and all aspects related to them. The store somehow always reminded me of the famous library burned down at Alexandria some two thousand years ago, with its countless scrolls. But this was a dingy dusty place as were so many of its old drawings, and I was always glad to get out into the daylight and fresh air again.

Of course I must also show my successor the Running Shed, dark, smoky and grimy as ever with its odours of steam locomotion, and all those magnificent resting giants ranged around in a great circle.

"All is not lost yet. I shall be coming back here," I promised myself, taking a lingering farewell from the all too familiar scene, as with a customary long hiss the resplendent *King Henry VIII*, No. 6013, eased itself majestically from the turntable, slid out through the main opening and up towards the Junction Station.

Beginning a trade— the A Shop

5

The dreaded message arrived on Thursday afternoon: "Tell Hugh Freebury to report to the AV Shop office at 8 o'clock next Monday morning."

It might have been worse. My overwhelming fear was to be sent to the V Shop, more commonly known as the Boiler Shop, where the real boilermaking was done. I had passed through it a few times on errands and the din was terrifying. Boilers seemed to be lying around everywhere, right way up, upside down or on their sides, and in various stages of construction or repair with men working away on most of them as if driven by demons. There were platers, the skilled men who laboriously shaped the thick steel plates for the shells or the copper plates for the fireboxes and assembled them, the drillers, drilling and tapping for the hundreds of steel or copper stays used to prevent distortion under intense heat, the riveters securing the various sections together with their riveting machines or pneumatic hammers and the red hot rivets, the 'stay bashers' rounding off the ends of the stays with a rhythmic staccato both inside and outside the fireboxes, and the caulkers sealing off all joints with their caulking tools to make sure steam and water would not escape.

The clammer of this unrelenting activity hit you like a gigantic hammer-blow itself the first time you passed through the door, bringing you up with a jolt. Although I was fascinated by the men on the huge rollers immediately in front of the Shop office, slowly but inexorably rolling the heavy conical sections of a Churchward tapered boiler into shape, requiring great experience and skill, I was always relieved to emerge into the sanity of the outside world again and its comparative calm, though the ears rang for some while afterwards.

There were two accepted hazards to a boilermaker's life. One was the 'boilermaker's deafness', caused by working for many years on, and especially inside, the locomotive boilers, for the incessant clangour of hammers on metal resounded again and 43

V Shop: reaming and tapping, January 1929

again on the hollow parts. It was acknowledged there was no need to shout in the tumult of the Boiler Shop because the tough industrious boilermakers had learned subconsciously to lip read or communicate with gestures, but once outside the confines of the workshop the facility seemed to desert them and a large number were quite hard of hearing.

The other hazard could be losing an eye and having to wear a glass one or a permanent black eye shade. The hammer and chisel were said to be the boilermaker's best friends and though the wearing of protective goggles when chipping or caulking was deemed compulsory, they were often dispensed with; and if a chip of steel—called "a bit of rag" in the trade—flew off the head of the tool it might well result in the loss of an eye. When such an accident occurred the First Aid men were instructed merely to pad the eye quickly and bandage it, then get the patient up to the Junction Station urgently, when the next express would be specially stopped to convey the unlucky victim to St. Mary's Hospital, Paddington, with the utmost speed. Several times in my boyhood I could remember my father coming home to impart the news: "'Nother boilermaker rushed up to London. Stopped the fast train. They think he'll lose an eye." All accidents in the Works, and they were not infrequent, were a serious topic which spread with remarkable rapidity amongst the men; and to remind boilermakers and others of this particular danger smashed goggles were set up in cases with a notice to the effect: "These goggles saved an eye. Always wear goggles and save your own."

So on the following Monday with my new overalls rolled up under my arm I climbed the high flight of wooden stairs to the AV Shop office and after giving my name to one of the clerks through the little sliding window was told to wait till the Foreman arrived. Some ten minutes later a sober-faced man in a grey suit and bowler hat appeared at the top of the stairs and strode along the verandah to his office without so much as a glance in my direction, to disappear inside.

There was another wait while the Foreman apparently dealt with the more pressing business of the morning and I looked down the long high Boiler Bay, as it was called, of the AV Shop. Below me was a tall black structure like a monolith whose purpose I couldn't work out, while beyond that were large steel frames in which boilers were placed and around which men were working special machines with counter-balance weights for ease of speed and operation. Looking down still further I could see an overhead crane with a similar large loco boiler hanging from its structure and being transported along, swaying slightly in the process. Just then the clerk tapped the window and motioned me to go into the Foreman's office.

For some reason I felt most uncomfortable in front of this stern man with firm jaw and tight mouth, seemingly more conscious of his influence and authority than the foremen of the PL Shop.

"Are you Hugh Freebury?"

"Yes—sir," I replied, not sure if this was the correct manner of address.

"H'm. And you want to be a boilermaker?"

At first I couldn't answer, for it wasn't true; and the Foreman looked up with an impatient stare.

"Well?"

I nodded nervously, feeling I daren't give a bad impression especially at such an early stage.

"I suppose you know most of the rules applying in the Factory. You've got to keep good time, not break those rules, and keep up your night school regularly. If you don't, you lose your apprenticeship. Is that clear? Learn to do what you're told—and keep out of trouble."

He reached for his phone and spoke through to the other office. "Take this boy down to the Checkie, then the Plating Chargeman." He handed me a piece of paper with a number on it. "This is your check number. Remember what I've told you."

I was escorted below by the office boy to the check board where an elderly round-shouldered little man was going along the hooks and marking down the numbers of the brass checks still hanging up.

"New lad here Walter," the office boy said. "And here's his check number."

Walter held it very close to his nose although he was wearing a very old pair of glasses.

"That's your check, there," he pointed. "You can't 'ave it now 'cause you'll be signed in this morning. Pick it up 'safternoon."

I was then taken down one side of the Boiler Bay past a long 45 row of fitters' benches, then through a gap three parts of the way down, back into the Bay itself to a large black cupboard where a tall individual was writing at the sloping top inside.

"I've brought you the new boy," my guide said, tapping on the door.

The Chargeman turned and studied me for a moment. "Ah, good. We've been waiting for you. I see you haven't got your overalls on yet, but it don't matter at the moment." He got up from his wooden seat, swung it inside and locked the door. "Now come with me, and watch your step."

Though apprehensive and rather overwhelmed by it all, I was surprised to be led away from the boilers into the AE Shop, then between two pits on which stood dirty, pathetic-looking engines without, among other things, their bogies, stepped over pipes, connecting rods and other fittings, until we reached the wide traversing table bay.

"Always be careful and look before you step down here," warned the Chargeman. "That traversing table down there goes quite fast, and though there's a bell on it the driver might not see you."

We crossed diagonally to the north corner of the huge Erecting Shop where long rust-red frames were standing, and I realised at once this was the New Work Section. It seemed most uncanny, because having been more or less obliged to settle for manual work on the shop floor it was the one place in the whole Works I would have chosen . . . But the relief was short-lived, for standing near a portable forge not much larger than a dust-bin stood three men, and I knew what was in store.

"Larry," called the Chargeman, "your new boy. Name's Hugh. Larry's in charge of the hand-riveting squad," he explained to me, "and he'll look after you."

Larry, a short, slightly tubby, elderly man with a rather sad face, stepped forward and shook my hand.

"Hello Hughie," he said, using the name I most disliked, and studying me up for a moment. "I think we'll get on all right by the looks of it. You're goin' to be our rivet 'otter."

So that really was to be my first job as an apprenticed boilermaker—heating up rivets! I was so downcast I almost felt like crying. Why had I so stupidly opted to come into the Factory at all, when some of my pals lower down at school now had reasonable jobs fixed up outside by the concerned and considerate Mr. Veness? No wonder boilermakers were looked down upon so often when they allowed their apprentices to do such menial work.

"You better 'ang yer jacket on that pillar over there and put yer overalls on," advised Larry. "Then I'll show you what to do."

But first I was introduced to the other riveter, a quiet, tight-lipped thin man, Fred Turney by name, who seemed almost deformed so rounded were his shoulders; and then the holder-up in dun overalls, Arthur Berresford, broader and taller than the others but with a square face and whitish doughy kind of complexion.

When ready to begin I was led to the forge which was already alight with small red coke.

"Now this under 'ere is your air," explained Larry Carter, pointing to a rounded stop-cock under the forge, "and you turn it on when you want to bring the fire up a bit. Not too much at once or you'll blow the fire all over the place. I always put the rivets in order on the floor and keep to that 'cause some of 'em are different lengths. This is your tongs for picking 'em up and you put the first in the middle of the fire like this, the second on the left and the third there, three at a time, see? Now we'll wait till they get 'otted up."

He turned on the air which was connected by means of an armoured flexible tube to a cock in the engine pit and soon the small fire began to brighten with flames appearing and fumes that soon began to tickle the back of my throat. With the long tongs Larry juggled around with the coke and rivets until the middle one was so hot it could hardly be distinguished from the glowing fuel.

"Now watch this careful-like," said Larry. "We want these rivets as 'ot as we can get 'em, but not burnt. Get hold of the rivet under the head and slowly twist it from side to side until we're ready. Then whip it out and pass it to Arthur. Move the next one to the middle and start over again. That's all there is to it."

He carried the white-hot rivet to the holder-up who was now in the pit under the locomotive frame. Arthur, who was wearing coarse leather gloves, picked up the rivet with much smaller 47 tongs, inserted it in the prepared hole and held it in place with the largest hammer I'd seen so far. Fred Turney, partly crouched on the other side behind a projecting bracket, immediately began flattening the glowing projecting end with crisp hammer blows, restricted though he was, finishing off the rivet with lighter and quicker taps.

Because everything was so new and strange that first morning went by quickly, though it was not without incident. I had some difficulty getting used to looking directly into the fire and twice lost rivets in the dazzling heat, sparks flying up in all directions as they began to 'burn' as foretold. There seemed more to it than at first thought because if you dripped them too much they wasted away and the shanks were too thin, while if the rivets were not hot enough they were tossed back at you contemptuously by the holder-up. On another occasion I was using my foot too violently to turn on the air and blew the fire open, shooting out small fire-balls in all directions and narrowly avoiding getting burnt.

As 12.30 approached I made my way back to the check board in the Boiler Bay where as soon as the Foreman left the men started to congregate. The Checkie had lifted up the swivel tray beneath and at the very first note of the hooter the brass checks flew from all directions into the tray and the men were off.

I walked right up through the long AM Shop where my father worked but had no intention of going home with him since most men thronging the streets before and after work strode along with a customary partner, but I also wanted to avoid any impression of being a 'Daddy's boy'. I shortly overtook my father, who had a steady gait because of suffering from rheumatism of the feet several years ago, and as soon as I arrived home my mother was anxious to know how I'd fared.

"Oh, it's all right Mam," I said, not wishing to give her more to worry about. "I'm just a rivet hotter, that's all. It's hot and dirty and dust from the coke gets in my hair, but I suppose I'll just have to put up with it for a while."

"It may not be for long," she tried to console me. "Go out in the kitchen and wash your hands."

"That reminds me Mam, have you got a small piece of soap, then I'll be able to wash my hands before I come home. And I'm going to leave my overalls in there if I can. I don't like coming out in them." She gave an understanding smile, as if she knew I was deserving of something better, and wished my father was a bit more forceful with other people. Because he was so easy-going she had to be the driving force as long as I could remember, and at times it had been hard work. He was a good husband in many ways, smoked a little when they couldn't really afford it, but only went to the Working Men's Club once a week at most, was patient—too patient at times—with us children and had never once struck her.

"Don't you think you should wear a cap at work Hugh?"

"No Mam, I think I'd look silly. And I don't care if they all laugh at me, I'm still going to wear my tie. It stops the dust from going down the front of my neck."

"Here's your father coming in. Let's get the dinner out."

I left for work that afternoon before my father because not only had I further to go, I wanted to time myself without hurrying. I'd been shown how to bank up the fire to save relighting it, and after lifting off my brass check made my way across the AE to my forge. Everyone sat around for at least five minutes after the last hooter, especially on the new work where they were so far away from the Shop office and would see the Foremen coming anyway.

It gave me time to study the huge AE Shop extension, as it was called, two long bays with massive overhead cranes each capable of lifting and transporting the heaviest 4-6-0s high above all the activity going on below. Most of the riveting on the new work was done by two hydraulic machines supported by chains from a swivel arm attached to a pillar, which could be lifted by the overhead crane and placed in appropriate places where the feed pipe to the machines could be connected to the water supply. One of these had long jaws for riveting the stays right down to the bottom of the engine frames, but the other was for smaller work. Any odd holes that the hydraulics couldn't reach had to be filled in by the hand-riveting squad.

There were about ten pits for new work, the first two generally occupied for marking out, where the frames would be laid flat on trestles for the skilled fitters to pore over the large drawings spread out before them, before deciding where the holes should be drilled for various internal and external parts making up the frame assembly. When this was done the heavy frame plates would be moved down to the pits of the other two new work 49

Chargehands, stood up in heavy round-based stands for the stays, internal cylinders and so on to be temporarily fixed and adjusted and then riveted in place. The remainder of the pits running down the workshop were allocated to the repair gangs, where engines would be stripped down partially or completely, parts renewed or repaired as required then eventually re-assembled.

The first sign of work resuming was when the crane driver started his amble along the runway of the goliath cranes. He was short and almost as round as a barrel, which no doubt accounted for his rolling gait, and I never understood why he left his crane some thirty or forty yards from the ladder leading up to the gantry unless it was the need for exercise at the prospect of being cooped up for long sessions in that suspended yellow box. He seemed an unusual man, humourless and quite detached, one reason perhaps he was chosen for the job, but as time went on I grew to admire his sharp eyesight from so high above, and his immaculate skill in handling the controls at his disposal. When his crane started rolling down the bay with an occasional crackle of sparks, the men began to bestir themselves and operations reluctantly began.

By the end of the afternoon I was becoming a little more accustomed to the practice of rivet hotting, though now and then one would come hurtling back because I'd mixed up the order of the rivets, or it was slightly 'nobbled' where I'd burnt it trying to do the job too well; or because, even after driving home the drift—a round tapered tool again called the boilermaker's 'friend' by the sarcastic fitters—the hole was not clear enough for the passage of the rivet.

I was immensely relieved when told to let the fire die out and work eased off all round. Most eyes were now on the AE Shop office waiting for the three Foremen to come down the steps for the last time that day; then there was a rush to the crude concrete troughs for the washing of hands. The riveters always pushed around their own sack truck laden with bags containing various hammers and other tools, and I got Larry's permission to hide my overalls amongst them for the night, before getting my small piece of soap and making my way to the nearest trough.

"Oh no you don't!" shouted one of the fitters aggressively, elbowing me out of the way. "Go and wash yer 'ands in the bucket!" He was referring to the large tin of water kept at the side of the forge for regularly cooling the tongs. Feeling very foolish and hurt, because no one had warned me, I walked back to do as he said.

"I thought they wouldn't let you get away with it," remarked Fred Turney, who had already washed in the bucket. "They're a funny lot, most of the fitters. Haven't you brought a towel? 'Ere, use this clean bit o' cotton waste, and bring a bit o' towel tomorra."

It was only when talking it over with my father that evening, I learned what was really behind it all. Some years previously the boilermakers had gone on a prolonged strike for more pay than the fitters, a 47 shillings a week basic as opposed to the fitters' 46, and when this was reluctantly and grudgingly conceded apparently the fitters were somewhat appeased with the offer of washing troughs with roller towels, not always changed as regularly as they might have been I noticed, and this privilege they intended to guard jealously. However later, depending in what part of the AE we were working, I found there were a few of these top artisans who had no objection to me washing my hands under their running water when they had finished, but I never ventured to use their hanging towels!

This was my earliest confirmation of what I'd previously heard of the pettiness, envy, divisions and strife often existing among working-class people; all in reality struggling for the same basic things in life—a few creature comforts, an occasional fleeting contentment if true happiness was never to be their lot, and a stability that ever seemed to elude them.

For such insecurity had been prevalent in our household as long as I could remember, a strained week-by-week existence that hinged completely on next Friday's pay packet which never lived up to expectations, and more usually proved to be less adequate even than hoped. Thus the dismal unending conflict went on, without any of our family going hungry, it's true, but an existence devoid of all but the basic necessities of living.

One day, come what may, I would break free from all this, gain some kind of security for myself and so be able to offer my caring parents a few little treats, perhaps even luxuries, now and then; failing that, at least some temporary relief from the pressing needs that ever seemed to be with them.   51

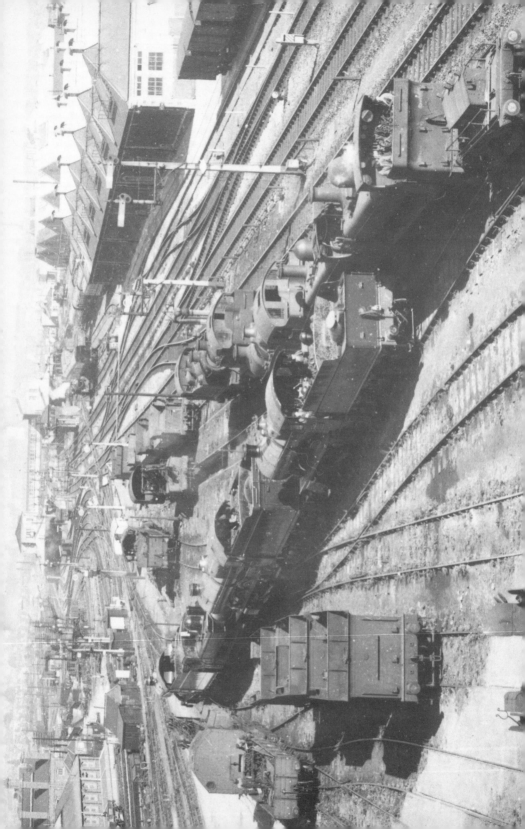

Injustice and a crucial test

6

In my earlier days at school I had two close friends. One, Eddie Wainwright lived in the same street and our parents were quite close since my mother did the weekly wash for Eddie's mother. The other pal had moved to Swindon from Gloucester, and when he first came to the school I immediately befriended him and we grew quite close. Ron Parker was a modest lad—a quality which has always attracted me—quite sporty and very intelligent, which was borne out when both he and Eddie gained scholarships, as they were called, and went off to the Secondary Schools of which there were three in Swindon, The College, Euclid Street and Commonweal. Of these Euclid Street was no more than an ordinary Elementary School in appearance and considered inferior, while Commonweal was looked upon as the choicest because it was a comparatively new building in the Old Town.

When Eddie went to Euclid Street and Ron to the College, I lost close contact with them until I was 15. Then a Christmas party brought Ron Parker and me together again and a firm friendship built up between us that lasted until we were in our 20s. I still admired Ron not only for his outstanding intelligence and cheerful manner but, in view of the snobbery amongst pupils of the Secondary Schools and particularly their parents towards the Elementary School population, his readiness to cut through this pretension amid the demands of his studies and devote a couple of get-togethers a week with a previous friend who was a mere boilermaker apprentice 'Inside'.

Mrs. Wainwright was inordinately proud of her younger son, regularly updating her acquaintances with his scholastic prowess, and knowing of the renewed friendship between myself and Ron Parker never hesitating to extol her son to the detriment of the unassuming "Parker boy" who, she perhaps intuitively felt, was more intellectual. This was clarified when the Schools Examination results were posted and Eddie had only managed to obtain what was then known as 'General Schools', while Ronald

53

Locomotives on parade, east end of Works

not only Matriculated but did so with Honours, the highest award given.

The question was now the future of the two boys. Mr. Wainwright, a fitter in the AE, and unlike his wife very mild-mannered, had no difficulty getting his son a post as a clerk in the Boiler Shop office with a prospect of getting on to the 9 o'clock Staff if he took further examinations.

Mr. Parker, a thin, short but smart-looking man with a narrow moustache, was a humble moulder, a first-class one for all that, in the J Shop or Iron Foundry, and after an interview and discussion with the redoubtable Clerk in the Managers' Office came away with the offer of an apprenticeship to fitting, turning and erecting for his son. He was so displeased he allowed his boy to go as a would-be trainee manager in an exclusive shoe shop in the Old Town; but when he subsequently heard of the post his son's contemporary had obtained he was so indignant that such blatant bias and prejudice should exist between fitters and all other tradesmen, that he sought another interview and plodded back up to the Managers' Office to make his feelings known. He was eventually shown into the inner sanctum and made to stand by the Clerk at the end of a long desk at which three others sat.

"I've come to you again about my son, Ronald Parker."

"Indeed," returned Mr. Wetherall imperiously, his morose features still studying the sheet before him. "You have decided to accept the apprenticeship I offered after all, then?"

"Indeed I haven't," was the prompt reply. "My boy is worth something better . . ."

"Well I'm sorry, there's nothing else available at present. You appreciate fitting is *the* trade, and the door to several other posts. Perhaps you will give it some more thought."

"I've given it plenty of thought since I was here last time." Alfred Parker kept his voice smooth but very firm. "And I would like you to explain something strange to me."

'Indeed, if I can."

"My boy, as you know from that sheet, took his School Certificate and Matriculated with Honours, getting five distinctions—five distinctions, mark you!"

"Yes, as you say I have all that written down here."

54   "Give me a moment please. His pal took the same exams and

got General Schools, and you know as well as me what that means. Now you explain to me why that lad's got taken on as a clerk in the Boiler Shop—you can have his name if you want—and all you can offer me for my lad is a workshop apprenticeship."

For once the dignified, imperturbable Clerk was thrown off balance; it was all the more discomfiting because his immediate colleagues would be listening though their heads might still be hung discreetly down.

"Well—er—we—er—take into consideration several factors, quite a number of things . . ."

"Such as the fact that his father's a fitter, and I'm only a moulder?" questioned Ron's father pointedly.

"No—no. I don't think that's the case at . . ."

"Oh, isn't it? Well I'm pleased about that, because what effect a father's job's got on his son's intelligence and capabilities I'll never be able to work out. Can you tell me what these factors are?"

"Well—um—length of service could be one. Er—perhaps loyal, that is, good service might be another . . ."

"Does that imply the service I've given the Company since I've been here might not be all it should be?"

"No, no!" protested Mr. Wetherall, feeling he wasn't extricating himself very cleverly from this increasingly embarrassing situation, and going back to his documents most diligently.

"Then let me make myself quite clear, Mr. Wetherall. If you're not able to offer my son at least a similar post to the one the other boy's got in the Boiler Shop, that is an office clerk's job, I'm going to take this further, right to the top if necessary, even if it costs me my own job. I hope I've made myself quite clear because that's exactly where I'm leaving it for the present, but I don't intend to be too patient in the matter. Thank you for seeing me Mr. Wetherall. I bid you good afternoon!" And with that Alfred Parker raised his right arm, turned about and walked purposively back to his work. Within the week Ronald was requested to attend Park House for medical examination, following which he was told to report to the L2 Shop office (ironically only a traversing table road separated it from the Boiler Shop) as a junior clerk on the 8 o'clock Staff.

I heard all this with the greatest relish, not only for my best friend's sake but because someone had at last challenged the system successfully. When I told my parents my mother immediately said: "And good luck to him! He deserves it. You should've stuck out like that for your own boy too, Harry."

"I did all I could," my father protested irritably. "It's that damn 40/- a week business. If I was on 42 bob I could've got something better for him. An' it's about time I got it anyway, even if I have bin on the same machine for ten years. Others have got it what've bin on one machine longer than me. Like Bill Watson. I know how he was made up; 'cause he's done a bit of lay preaching up at the Railway Mission where our Head Foreman goes. That's 'ow he got it."

"Never mind all that, let's think of our Hugh at the moment," my mother reminded him.

"Yes Dad," I put in. "Please go down and see about my name again."

"I was down there only a couple of months ago . . ."

"Twelve weeks," my mother corrected him quickly.

"All right, twelve weeks. An' they told me there was still a waiting list as long as your arm, and we'd have to be patient."

"We've been patient Dad. My name's been down there for over a year now. Please go down again. I hate rivet hotting. I'm not learning anything, not even boilermaking."

"Are you still quite sure you want to go down the Running Shed Hugh?" asked my mother, to my surprise.

"Yes, of course. Why?"

She smiled patiently at me before going on.

"Your father had another chat with Mr. Gorton the other day and he still thinks we're unwise to let you go down there. I suppose he should know. The medical examinations are quite stiff especially for colour blindness, and if you get ruptured you're out for good."

"I know Mam. I've been in to all that."

"But d'you realise," put in my father, "what a hard job it is when you get on, shovelling all that coal—three or four tons of it on a long run."

"We only want to make sure you're going into it with your eyes wide open," added my mother. "We don't want you to finish up as a boiler washer or ash-pan cleaner, which happens to some of them. And it's all hours of the day and night."

"It's no good Mam, I've made up my mind. Anything's better than what I'm doing, anybody can do it. But it's not just that. I really do want to go on the footplate. Really Mam."

"All right Harry," she turned to him. "Perhaps you ought to go down again and try to push it. I don't think we're going to be able to talk him out of it."

"I only wish I could." My father, I'm sure, considered he'd been there enough already and felt awkward going anyway, but hadn't the courage to say so outright.

Next day he made the journey yet again to No. 19 office. I could picture the faces of both clerks clouding as he walked in, still in grubby slop and overalls. This is how I further imagined the scene.

"Sorry to bother you again, but I've come to see if there is hope of my boy being called up yet."

The senior one might try to conceal his impatience and suppress a sigh.

"I thought I told you last time we would be getting in touch if we required him. H'm! Wait a moment."

He would rise with measured dignity, I could imagine, go to the filing cabinet, extract a folder and study it carefully.

"Yes, just as I thought. His name's still here. He's only just turned 16, according to this, so there's plenty of time yet. What is he doing at present?"

"Well, I've got him apprenticed to boilermaking. Of course, he's not happy with it. Still got his mind dead set on the Running Shed."

"Yes, and so have lots of others. Which workshop is he in?"

"The AV, down the new shop."

"I see." The Clerk might appear to write something on the sheet, then look up again at the diffident workman before him. "We still can't promise anything. Once taken on it's a secure job if they keep in good health, so naturally we have lots of good applicants. You must leave it with me to see what can be done. If he is wanted, I tell you again, we will get in touch with you."

"Thank you very much," my father would say, relieved I know to be free again of the precise uncomfortable atmosphere of the 57 office block. As the door firmly closed I could sense the Senior Clerk pondering before returning the folder to the cabinet and resuming his seat.

"I think I'm getting rather tired of the sight of that individual walking in here so often. What might we do about it?"

During the brief interview I'm sure his colleague would have been thinking along similar lines.

"I have an idea that might possibly work. But we'll need to get the co-operation of Park House."

A fortnight later to my immense joy I was requested to attend the Medical Examination Centre at Church Place known to so many working for the G.W.R. not only in Swindon but throughout the system, for all drivers and firemen especially must present themselves there regularly for their periodical check-up. I decided to take the afternoon off so that I could appear in my best clothes and give a favourable impression.

As I sat alone in the waiting-room my heart pounded away in spite of the effort to get a grip on myself. This was the moment I'd planned and hoped for since that memorable experience five years ago of first mounting the footplate, and I mustn't fail at this last crucial stage.

Presently a door opened and a well-groomed official smiled briefly at me and beckoned.

"Come here lad," he said, a little surprised, I hoped, at the clean, alert 16 year-old who immediately jumped to his feet; perhaps a little different from many who came! "Follow me."

We went along a short corridor and entered a room lined with glass-doored cupboards resting on wide benches.

"Now you do realise," began this man, "you have to be perfectly fit as an engine driver or fireman, and keep in good health?"

"Yes sir," I replied. "I've never been seriously ill."

"Good. But you realise also it's not an easy job, particularly as a fireman, and a dirty one too."

I nodded.

"All right. Now stand just here. I'm going to cover your left eye and I want you to read the letters over there as far down as you can." I did so without difficulty and the test was repeated for the other eye. "That's satisfactory. Now go over to my colleague."

He was waiting with a sheet of variable sized print pasted on a small board with a handle, which he passed to me.

"Hold it this far from your eyes, and read off what it says."

Except for the very last line which was minute, I read it clearly.

"Now come across here." He took me to a tray containing short pieces of varied-coloured wools alongside which was a second tray divided into partitions, one different coloured wool in each division.

"From all those colours," he instructed me, "I want you to pick out six of each that match these separate ones in the smaller tray. Do you understand? It's very important."

There were varying shades of red—from pink to crimson—light and dark greens, pale to deep yellows, all intermingled. The basic colours were easy to distinguish, but as I progressed it became more difficult and confusing. Eventually I looked up feeling slightly uneasy with my effort, which the clerk studied gravely.

"H'm!" he grunted. "I don't like the look of some of these. Perhaps you'd better try again."

With this the other man hurried across and sifted through the wools in the three divisions.

"Oh, they will do," he concluded, staring at his companion. "It's not a bad effort. Obviously he's not colour blind. That's over for you, but the next part is very critical."

He opened a cupboard beneath the bench top and withdrew a long narrow vessel like a large test tube.

"I want you to go in the toilet over there," he pointed, "and pass a sample of your water in this for us to analyse."

He led me to the door and stood near it making sure it was left ajar, which I found rather embarrassing, adding to my difficulty in producing any specimen at all, since I'd made certain of attending to that part of nature at the public toilets opposite before entering the building. My attention was further diverted by the voices of the two clerks as they loudly conversed.

"Oh yes," one was saying, "it's the very thing that lets a lot of them down."

"And you can understand," added the other. "After all it's vital. So much depends on it."

"I couldn't agree more. Just suppose he was taken giddy on the footplate. It could be disastrous, and not only for himself."

"Well, he seems a fairly intelligent lad. I'm sure he's sensible enough to realise other people's lives would be in jeopardy. How are you getting on in there?"

"I'm not quite ready yet," I replied without turning. "I went just before I came."

"Keep trying," was the injunction. "We must have something to work on."

Their words had made me more anxious and less inclined than ever, but after much further strain I managed to deposit about half an inch of liquid in the chemistry jar, and adjusting my clothes walked out rather sheepishly and handed it over.

"Well," said the senior man, studying the sample closely, "that certainly looks thick. Do you have any giddy turns?" I shook my head. "You're quite sure? All right, that's all for today. You may go now."

It was a very confused and subdued Hugh Freebury who pensively walked back home. Everyone knew railway clerks carried much sway in the Works but the Running Shed was not under control of the Factory, being part of the Bristol Engineering Division, yet those two men seemed to be very responsible. Why hadn't I been examined by the doctor?

My mother listened carefully to my story and said we must wait and see what my father thought of it when he came home later.

"Seems a bit queer to me," he remarked when I told him. "Would've thought you'd gone before the doctor first. We'll have to wait and see."

"Have you ever had any trouble with your water, Hugh?" asked my mother casually, certain she would have known had it been so.

"Not really Mam. I remember once I was in the lavatory in the park and an old man looked over at me and said: 'That's some mighty thick stuff—too yellow. Want to drink more water my boy, flush those kidneys out a bit more.' I always try to now."

Both my parents burst into laughter at this and I smiled too, seeing them so genuinely amused for a change. Nevertheless the matter weighed heavily with me throughout the next few days, and those hopes of achieving my burning ambition began to fade more and more. Within the week the Shop office boy sought me out saying the Foreman was waiting to see me upstairs.

60   I mounted those wooden steps with a thudding heart, not only

because of tension at confronting that gentleman again, but apprehension of what I was about to hear from him.

"I thought you came here as an apprentice boilermaker," he greeted me bluntly. Somehow without that bowler hat his receding hair made him look much less formidable.

"Yes," I nodded. I just couldn't bring myself to say "sir".

"Then this seems strange. There's a letter here saying you wanted to be taken on down the Running Shed."

"Yes. I've had my name down for some time."

"Why?" I felt as if I had exceeded my rights, or committed some serious offence.

"I—I thought it might be a bit more secure. You don't get the sack at 21."

"So that's what it's all about." He pointed again to the letter in front of him. "Well it says here, after your first test you're not up to the standard expected. So your name's been taken off the list. D'you understand? Is that quite clear?"

"Y—yes," I could just manage to stammer.

"All right. That's all. You can go."

Though I knew the eyes of the workers immediately below the office—the men on the shears and punching machines—were watching me, speculating why I'd been 'called up on the carpet', I couldn't conceal my abject disappointment. Much as I'd tried to stifle all presentiments following that strange conversation intended I felt sure for my hearing in Park House, now they'd proved true I felt shattered, as if my whole world was collapsing around me. Now I was fully convinced I'd been unfairly treated, but why, for what reason I might never know. I knew of an engine cleaner who'd been taken on only recently and who was well below me at school; so it could hardly be my level of intelligence that had let me down. Perhaps they thought I didn't look strong enough, or wouldn't fit in. Whatever the reason, it was definite and final.

Mr. Parker, Ron's dad, had been forthright and courageous enough to defy a system that was governed not by what you were and what you were capable of, but what job your father did; and had shamed the men who enforced this system. My father, lovable though he was, had neither the forceful personality nor the firm grounds for changing my future, consigned as I now was to 61 boilermaking for the next five years at least, much as I resented the prospect and dreaded it. Fate was cruel to me and remorseless, especially when within myself I felt capable of better things and would have strived my very utmost to be worthy of them.

Fashioning boiler mountings, January 1936

Workshop procedures

7

"Never mind Hugh, it may be all for the best," said my mother, ever ready to sense my mood. "You know the old saying: 'When one door closes another opens, if you look for it'. There's something in that."

"Yes Mam, I've heard you say it before. I'm not so sure. But don't worry about me, I'll be all right."

"Of course you will my boy," father tried to encourage me. "Just have faith and it will all work out right in the end. Some boilermakers have done very well in the world. Did you know one of them became Chancellor of Liverpool Cathedral? There's no knowing what you'll do when you get on a bit."

Even if such things irritated each time I heard them, I had no desire to give my parents any worry that could be avoided, especially my dear mother. Consequently, though when alone I occasionally let my feelings get the better of me with this sense of frustration, outwardly I gave the impression to my family that I'd risen above it all.

Clearly, once you'd mastered the practice of heating rivets to the satisfaction of your mates there was no challenge whatever in it, yet I realised I could be less fortunate. First of all, the pay. Though basically only marginally better than when I was an office boy, there was that prospect of 'balance' once a fortnight. This varied from gang to gang, but since my Chargehand was a particular favourite of the Foreman who was supposed to decide the price for all the various jobs, with a Piecework Inspector to check these, our gang usually did well with an average of 50% balance every other week.

This completely eclipsed the balance earned by the Planers' Gang of my father, the worst paid in the AM Shop which was lucky to get 10 or even 5%, and was often 'in debt'. This meant the men hadn't earned their basic wages over the fortnight and the Head Foreman had somehow to 'work the books' until the next two-weekly period, when they must try to put things right, but 63 sometimes went even further into debt. When the time-sheets of 'balance week' came into the workshops there was great keenness by men and boys to know what was due before the stoppages were deducted. These amounted to very little in my case, only a few pence a week for the G.W.R. Medical Fund Society, set up by the Company for the benefit of its employees.

The paying-out procedure itself was similar all over the factory to that of the PL Shop, the black table being set out in a convenient place and the men lining up in check order to be paid. Unlike some, our Foreman seemed to wait until the very last moment before making his entry to the pay-out scene. The first dozen or so men would be already in line with all the others hanging round in readiness, and as the minutes ticked by the odd man would look up to the office and say: "Come on you awkward old bugger. Time's getting on." For everyone was supposed to be paid in Company time and our supervisor could arrange it precisely so that the last man picked up his pay tin just as the hooter started its blast, almost to the second of 12.30.

While as an office boy I could go forward and pick up my tin before all the others, here in the AV of course I was always on edge, frightened I would miss my turn, so searched anxiously for the couple of men before or immediately after me in the queue, and having found them must not lose sight of them until we were in place; because if you missed your turn you were forced to wait until all the rest were paid out before getting your tin, and be subjected to a freezing glare or even rebuke from the Foreman. I never missed my turn, but had a few narrow squeaks in the first few weeks when I mistook someone else for my 'marker'. And of course, once the Pay Clerk had slammed down the lid of the metal case containing unclaimed tins it was sealed and not opened again until safely back in the Pay Office, a special chit from the Foreman being required to claim it.

So each week on the way home after checking my earnings with the pay-slip I was calculating how much of my pocket money I could put to one side for the special treat I was planning for my mother. This was to come later, for although I paid her something for my keep and relieved her of the burden of buying my clothes, she insisted on not wanting to "make anything" from me and

64 began paying weekly instalments of 2/6d a week on a handsome

bicycle of my own choice, not the common Hercules model but an aristocratic Raleigh Roadster, with chrome butterfly handlebars, three speed gear and oil bath. It saved me among other things the long walk to the College evening classes and enabled me to explore the countryside all round, particularly the Wiltshire Downs and nearby Berkshire villages throughout lighter evenings and week-ends, often accompanied by my only close friend Ron Parker.

Another small advantage of being with the hand-riveting squad was that at least I moved around, not only on the new work but in other parts of the AE Shop. The monotony of working for the hydraulic squads was worse than anything I experienced, for the rivets would be thrown down in piles to be picked up mechanically by the boy and cast into the fire with little judgement required about the correct heat, often a cherry red being sufficient, and to stand there for a long run just lifting the rivets in and pulling them out like an automaton would have sent me crazy. "You're lucky to be on that squad," the others would say to me. "At least you get a bit of variety. How about a change for a week?"

It was not only moving more than they did around the new work bays, but when the near-completed locos were moved to the bottom end of the workshop near the main doors for finishing off, there was often still odd hand-riveting to be done, and here it was cleaner, quieter and more relaxing. Then every couple of months or so the forge and all the gear would be moved up to the east end of the older part of the huge building where it was quietest of all, and our assignment was to rivet a complete new front end for a 2900 class, that type so popular for its easy performance, but which after 20 years or so was showing strain and even cracks in the extension frames.

Rather than repair the latter it was found to be almost as cheap to build up a new unit of outside cylinders, extension frames and curved front ends. It amounted to a lot of varied work for the squad but most of all I was interested in watching them secure the buffer beam with its 7/8in. snap-head rivets which must be white-hot for the operation. First they were roughed down by alternate quick hammering, then one riveter grabbed the snap while the other picked up the sledgehammer at his side. The snap tool was 65 held over the still glowing nobbled end and driven home with swinging blows of the sledge until the required shape was formed. Larry had an attractive easy rhythm which even the fitters admired, but Fred Turney had a crouching laborious style which seemed to require so much more of a physical effort and several more blows than Larry's to accomplish the task.

Another attraction of this corner away from all the hustle was the proximity of the Stationary Engine Plant, sometimes officially called the Home Trainer, a huge arrangement of wheels and belts and gauges first designed by the Great Man himself and constructed in a rectangular pit so that locomotives in steam could be backed onto it with their driving wheels in contact with those of the plant. When the locomotive was firmly anchored (sometimes an 0-6-0 tank engine would be brought up at the front end for added security) she would be started up and her speed raised to whatever was necessary for the test, her fuel and water consumption being monitored throughout, together with the functioning of any parts under review.

A large gauge registered her speed and at 60 m.p.h. plus there was considerable vibration, while it was fascinating to see the fireman working all out to feed the hungry firebox as if on a long run, and the driver in his place notching her up with the motion, piston valves, pistons, crossheads, connecting rods and driving wheels operating so amazingly fast it was difficult to detail them; while all the time the bogie wheels might be idle! Each time the squad came up to work on a 29 front-end I hoped the plant would be in use, but I was not often lucky and had to content myself with another walk all round the great pit studying its design with a keen interest.

There was another unusual section near this end of the immense workshop. Two lesser known occupations concerned with locomotive work were that of plasterer and bricklayer! The former was engaged on lagging, covering the boiler barrels with a thick coat of what looked like white plaster, but was basically asbestos mixed with water. I was led to believe that for some reason, like that of the coppersmith, it wasn't considered a very healthy job. I could believe it, for when the men had been working for a while and their overalls, faces, hands and boots were covered in a kind of fluffy white dust, there was certainly a

66

ghost-like appearance about them. When the lagging was thoroughly dry the cleaders came along with their thin rolled-steel sheets, wrapping them round the boilers and securing them with adjustable straps.

The bricklayer was one of the last to work on the locomotive before it left the workshop. His particular contribution was to build up a brick arch of specially shaped firebricks inside the firebox to deflect the gases and ensure efficient circulation. He needed to be a fairly small man to wriggle in and out through the round, none-too-large fire hole with his hands above his head; and I, for one, didn't envy him in the least such a livelihood.

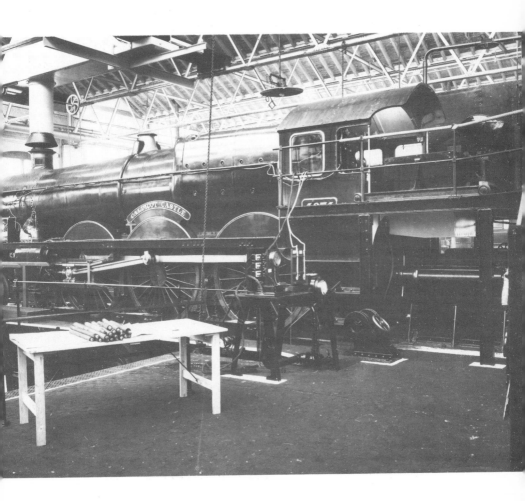

Caldicot Castle *on test plant, February 1929*

Taboos 8

Throughout the whole railway works of those days there were two emphatic taboos, eating lunch and smoking. The latter never concerned me though several of the men were often so desperate for a 'draw' they would take chances of getting caught. Many used the large overhead conveniences where before entering you were obliged to hand in your brass check, its number and the time surrendered being recorded to avoid abuse. Sometimes when I put a heap of damp coke on the forge and blue smoke and fumes rose towards the roof an impulsive workman would suddenly appear, light up and blow a few puffs into the ascending column in the hope his misdemeanour would be undetected, knowing that the vigilant Foremen were always on the look-out for the tell-tale thin wisps. The penalty for being caught was inevitable—sent home for two, or even three, days for a first offence.

Taking a mid-morning break was also forbidden, particularly the eating of lunch, as it was called, which most workers ate as surreptitiously as possible around 10 o'clock of a morning. Some even indulged in brewing a can of tea, using the nearest forge for the boil-up. Indeed one story went the rounds concerning the Head Boilermaker Foreman, who was a fitter by trade and disliked for that alone by those under him, coming unexpectedly on an unattended forge in the AE Shop with a can of water coming up to the boil on the fire. The shrewd and unpopular Foreman decided to stand with his back to the fire and wait, knowing the offender whoever it might be had probably gone off to fetch the tea for his brew and would either have to reveal himself or allow his can to boil dry.

But the astute boilermaker, it so happened, refused to be humiliated by his scheming overseer, and since the forge was standing near an engine pit, got a hazel rod (often called a withy and used as a kind of shock-absorbing handle when twisted round a snap or set tool) and slid quietly into the pit under the locomotive frame. Carefully and coolly he manoeuvred the end of 69

Lydford Castle *on traverser, June 1936*

the rod under the wire handle of the tea can then slowly swung it round to the edge of the pit. When securely in his grasp he crawled along under the engine frame and climbed out triumphantly at the other end.

With his back still towards the forge the Head Foreman finally decided it was time the can had boiled dry, but when he turned to survey the damage his vigil had caused, his sneer rapidly changed from disbelief into anger; and he stamped away savagely to the great glee of those who, discreetly hidden, had witnessed the whole incident and saw it as another success in the constant battle of wits between authority and the manual workers over the enforcement of Factory rules.

Following my disenchantment at being turned down for the Running Shed and the somewhat cynical attitude of my Foreman, I found myself less able to respect the latter and his ways. He regularly strolled around the AE Shop at least twice a day, stopping now and then with feet apart and giving some impression at gossiping, but with alert eyes moving all round. Invariably he was accompanied by his loyal lieutenant Bob Thatcher, one reason for this attachment being that the latter was brought down from the Boiler Shop by the Foreman and given control of the Plating Gang without having any previous experience of such work. This particular move had been over the head of the well-established leading hand Sid Matthews, who'd considered himself a certainty for the vacancy. Matthews himself, however, was not always held in the best esteem by other workmates and, perhaps understandably in the circumstances, would drop an occasional unsupportive remark regarding his new Chargehand.

But I found Bob Thatcher quite fair in most things, though the man's submissiveness towards his Foreman seemed out of character, being a fine figure of a man, tall and upright and quite alert. Sometimes so eager would he be to join the Foreman on those regular jaunts the Chargehand might be seen scurrying along the workshop to catch up with him, then give a double shuffle to fall into step at his side. Yet no one suggested they socialised. I had been told, for instance, many a Friday night in the private bar of a certain pub in the Old Town the Foreman could be found with certain followers around him and never without an empty glass to ensure they continued in his favour. Whether this was just sour grapes or not I was never able to determine. But to his credit, there was never a report that the favourite Chargehand had been seen amongst them.

But one of these regular supporters was a holder-up who held the lightest and easiest job in the Boiler Bay. This was riveting together the engine cabs that were assembled one at a time on the special jigs by Sid Matthews, another clean light job probably gained as compensation for losing the position of Chargehand. The largest hot rivets used were a mere ⅜in. diameter, heated on the forge by means of a perforated plate so that they would not be lost in the gleaming fire, with lots of smaller cold riveting to be done as well, and the team was made up of a young lad as a rivet hotter and a so-called boilermaker apprentice theoretically in charge. But other than the Foreman this holder-up was a near law unto himself, even his Chargehand treated him with circumspection. He could be seen up in the Shop office almost every day in deep conversation and for this was looked upon with some suspicion; some workmates pitying him, some resenting him, while others may have exaggerated his influence and played up to him.

When the Foreman went on those rounds his gait was rarely a purposeful one like most of his bowler-hatted fraternity. Whether it was deliberate or not I could never tell, but he gave the impression of hoping to catch someone off guard, which inevitably put all boilermakers and their mates on their mettle when the message flashed along ahead that he was on his way. He might come up to one of them with some query or criticism; or even make some comment intended as a joke at which the recipient would dutifully laugh. But should the vast majority err in any way and be caught, say, surreptitiously smoking or stealing a bite of lunch of a morning they could expect no compassion—rather a strict summary punishment.

So perhaps in this respect I was fortunate one morning when our squad had broken off for a break while in the process of riveting the bunker on a 5700 tank engine moved down to the quiet bottom end of the AE. In the winter some men, including fitters, might come along and toast their sandwiches on the fire of the rivet hotters, and I soon followed the practice. On 71 this particular occasion after toasting my lunch I climbed into the cab to enjoy it, looking out over the bunker up the long workshop. It not only tasted good, but must have smelt it too, for a face suddenly appeared from nowhere at the cab opening.

"Come and have a look at this Thatcher!" rasped the Foreman's voice with somewhat of a hint of satisfaction.

For a moment I was completely paralysed. The Foreman's face disappeared to be replaced by the Chargeman's

"What d'you think you're doing up there?" he demanded. "Come down here at once."

I left my lunch on the ledge and scrambed down with legs like jelly and face white as death. The Foreman gave me a contemptuous glare.

"What you got to say for yourself?"

I could only shake my head, speechless under his withering stare.

"You know you're not allowed up there!" He turned to his Chargeman. "That's his one and only warning. Next time he'll get sent out for a week!" With that he turned away and strode off, leaving his companion to catch him up and perhaps apologise; and the culprit feeling quite sick! About half an hour later the Chargeman returned and called me away from the forge.

"Why on earth did you let yourself get caught like that?" he asked me quietly.

"I—I don't know," I stammered. "I—I thought somebody would have warned me you were coming. They usually do."

"Don't you always rely on that," he advised me, taking I thought a little pity on a sensitive apprentice, one perhaps not quite such a hard case as some others. "Now just be more careful in future, or I'm afraid you'll really get sent home you know."

"Yes, I understand." I further understood why I received no real reprimand for having brought lunch into the Works, since on more than one occasion I'd seen him eating his own from the drawer of his tall black box, at which he sat near the customary time (10 a.m.) with the door pulled-to as much as possible!

However this resolved me never to be caught again like that. Next morning at breakfast when my father was cutting the sandwiches I said: "Don't do any for me, Dad. I'm going to try to do without lunch in future."

72

"Oh, and why's that then, my boy?"

"Well I don't always feel like it, and sometimes it puts me off my dinner."

"You got to keep up your strength you know," was all my father said, and I was relieved, because I couldn't bring myself to tell the full truth at that stage. But a couple of days later when my mother questioned me on the matter I admitted I'd been caught by the Foreman and threatened I'd be sent out next time.

"Don't let it bother you like that," she advised me. "We knew the family when they lived in this part of the town before he was ever made Foreman. They went to our church regularly until he was made up, then moved to Old Town. But it's not worth bothering you with the whole story because nobody can do anything about it."

"That's quite right," confirmed my father. "It goes on all the time, this keeping in with the right people. But don't let it stop you trying to get on Hugh. Keep up your night school I say, and that'll always stand you in good stead."

There the matter was laid to rest as far as my parents were concerned, but certainly not in my mind. I'd heard quite a lot about influence already and "not what you know, but who you know" from men in the workshop, and was beginning to realise how often this seemed to operate, part of a system which afforded little hope to someone like me.

Furthermore, I learned from the other rivet hotters there was no possibility of being taken off the forge until your 18th birthday, when you became due for the 'big rise' so that the riveters couldn't earn your wage and their balance too. More often you were then transferred to the boiler bay for a long session at 'stay bashing', knocking down the ends of the copper stays which supported the firebox and outer casing of the largest boilers—smaller ones were repaired in the V Shop—and this perhaps even on the hateful night shift!

But one thing in my favour I was determined to exploit to the full when the time came. I attended night school at the College in Victoria Road three times a week, one more than the bare minimum set down, and unlike many of my fellow apprentices kept up a regular attendance. Many of my trade hated theoretical study, and though it may seem unkind weren't up to it anyway, 73 seeing no point in requiring to know more than was necessary to carry out their daily chores in the workshops. In consequence they might put in an appearance every other week, even less if they could get away with it, that is until a report filtered back through the channels, resulting in being 'called up on the carpet' for a confrontation with the Foreman. Even this did little to intimidate the tougher cases, country lads who lived some miles out in such places as Highworth, Chiseldon or Wootton Bassett, for night school then meant getting home after ten o'clock of an evening, even if there was transport.

So for these unfortunate lads there was little else than to be consigned again to unpleasant repetitive jobs like cutting off rivets and stay-ends with the heavy pneumatic guns, centre-punching for the drillers, and after that dismantling the dirty burnt copper fireboxes and cleaning out the waterways. Since perhaps instead of rivet hotting some of these had already spent a long while with the drillers, sitting inside the fireboxes and passing back the long taps which threaded the hundreds of holes for the stays supporting that most vulnerable part of a locomotive, their experience by the time they reached 21 did not leave much to boast about.

If only to keep myself out of the boiler bay as long as possible I was determined to take my father's advice and keep up my studies. Often after the 8½ hour day I felt too tired and was tempted to relax at home, particularly if the weather was unfavourable, but though there was no pressure brought to bear on me in this respect from my parents, I forced myself to go.

Also, I soon felt an instinctive desire for knowledge, now realising more than ever the limitations my elementary education had inflicted on me. In the hope of making up for that great gap I put aside a regular amount of pocket money each week to buy the bargain books offered by the popular press, books at prices the ordinary man could afford and representing excellent value. In this way I gradually acquired a modest little collection covering a wide variety of subjects, and found I could teach myself from them quite comfortably.

Then I looked forward so much to those long week-end walks with my clever friend, Ron Parker, who patiently taught me the rudiments of French, physics and more advanced grammar, so that pursuing these things from my books became that much easier. It gave me the edge I wanted over my fellow apprentices, and a quiet but determined resolve to better myself no matter what obstacles lay ahead.

Trip holidays

9

Early in April each year on all shop notice boards appeared preliminary information regarding the Works annual holiday— Trip. The announcement gave the date of the event—it always began on the first Friday in July—and a request for all members of the Mechanics Institute to attend the main building in Emlyn Square for membership cards to be endorsed for the year. A few weeks later would follow information for completing the forms of application for the free pass for members and their families to any destination on the Great Western system. This concession alone amply repaid the small fee for membership deducted from most wage packets, since almost everyone saw the advantages of subscription although it was only voluntary.

For instance, there were other commendable facilities available to members. Swindon in common with many other towns was without a public library, but in its main building the Institute had an extensive collection of books covering a wide variety of topics readily on loan to members' families. The large, impressive building with its twin towers on the north side also contained an elaborate reading room with an official always on guard to ensure only members were admitted, and if you were not a frequent visitor it was advisable to carry your card on you. Here on large sloping desks were all the daily and evening papers and popular magazines, such as the *Illustrated London News, The Strand Magazine, The Sketch, The Tatler* and so on. Other premises were situated in Rodbourne and Gorse Hill with similar facilities but on a smaller scale.

On the upper floor of the main building was also the reasonably-sized Playhouse which repertory companies or local amateurs might hire. I had once performed on the stage—as the front part of a donkey! It was a school production of the musical *Don Quixote* and was completely sold out on the three nights it was presented and had a favourable write-up in the *Evening Advertiser*. Both my parents were proud to be in the audience   77

The Reading Room, Mechanics' Institute with the nameplate of Royal Sovereign, *July 1938* since Jane appeared as one of the ladies of Castille; but father was particularly impressed to see his Head Foreman only a few seats away enjoying to the full the antics of Sancho Panza's 'Dapple' with myself, his own boy, pulling the strings in the head of the costume donkey!

Some time in May, Trip application forms giving the details of numbers in each family travelling, the destination and date of return journey must be handed in so that the great exodus could be meticulously planned. Then the final visit to the Institute a few days before the mass departure resulted in the issuing of passes and leaflets detailing the special trains to be run and any other essential information, such as where to change and the times for getting to other destinations where the specials did not run.

Those resorts in the south-west, Dawlish, Teignmouth, Paignton and Penzance were always popular as well as Weston-super-Mare for day trippers, but Weymouth was favoured above all, sometimes requiring up to five special trains and consequently known as "Swindon-by-the-Sea". Most employees could only afford the excursion on Trip Day, for the ensuing week was a lock-out, as it was called, without pay and that needed to be taken into account as well as the day out. Those who were lucky enough to be slightly better paid or had no children to consider might opt for a week perhaps further afield, Tenby in Wales often warranting its own special train.

Our own little family had once relished this exceptional luxury some years previously when the Works were on full time, and it meant travelling overnight from the Junction Station precluding those long restless hours in bed when you were sure your parents were oversleeping and would not be up in time. We had stayed in a very ordinary house quite close to the Atlantic Ocean with room and attendance, which meant you provided all the food for your family but it was prepared and cooked by the landlady, who accommodated you in the required number of bedrooms plus the use of a dining-room. It was the week of a lifetime, marred only by the return journey.

If your resort was a terminus, such as Weymouth, the coaches would be waiting and you could queue up well beforehand to ensure comfortable seats; but if you had to wait on the station platform for the train's arrival it could be a frightening experience, especially for small children. Long before time every available space would be filled with some families well spread out to stand more chance of grabbing a door handle, for though officials said a seat was provided for everyone it was often proved untrue, with some Trippers having to sit on their luggage throughout the non-stop journey.

Tenby platform was packed well in advance as usual and when the 'special' eventually crawled in some individuals snatched the brass door handles and walked along with the train until it stopped, blocking the entrance to the compartment until the rest of the family came up and piled in. On this occasion father was fortunate, not being as active on his feet as most, for a compartment door stopped within easy reach, but just as his hand encountered the handle a ruthless character dashed along brushing his arm clear and pushing my father into the rest of us standing there.

One or two scuffles with accompanying curses had already broken out along the train accompanied by screams from terrified children, but my father was no match for this resolute roughneck and could only stand by as the entry was blocked for all but the other's kith and kin. We had no alternative but to follow in behind only to discover, as we feared, every compartment in that coach full or nearly full and settle down dejectedly on our luggage in the corridor for the seven-hour journey.

My mother was furious with father for letting the usurper get away with it so easily.

"Why didn't you go for him Harry?" she demanded angrily.

"Well, I wasn't expecting it. He took me by surprise."

"At least you could have choked him off. You was there first."

"I know," conceded Dad, "but what was the point. It was only wasting time."

"Wasting time or not," went on my mother, "you never stick up for us when you ought to. Sometimes I can't make you out."

Then she realised she was upsetting her children still further, for it was an unusual outburst from her, a spontaneous reaction directed more towards the other man than her husband. Eventually by walking along we came across odd places in compartments not too far apart so that we were able to keep in contact with an occasional sandwich, orange or drink of water, the 79 latter always presenting a problem on these long non-stop journeys with no buffet facilities.

But that Trip Week was an exception and when short time was reintroduced—no Saturday morning work and sometimes a further day out as well—it meant the vast majority would become Day Trippers only. Well before dawn on that long-awaited morning the dark streets began to echo to the trample of feet and subdued sounds of excited children all making their way to the railway sidings where lines of carriages had been shunted and labelled the day previously. To gain access to these an odd workman or so would be around with a short ladder for climbing up into the compartments, and by coming along quite early a family could choose where they wished to sit, though the children would be restless, waiting for the bump of the engine being attached, soon after which the journey would begin.

After progressing for a few miles dawn would break across the countryside and speculation begin as to what kind of weather might be awaiting them all at their destination. Cows lying down in the passing fields were a sign of rain, father said, with his knowledge of rustic lore gained from his early years on the farm, but if the majority were standing it was going to be fine.

Most Trippers reached their destinations before the resorts came alive, especially the overnight travellers, but the day visitors made their way direct to the beach to secure a favourable spot and sit it out most of the day. I could recall a day trip to Teignmouth when very heavy rain greeted us on arrival, which meant heading straight for the pier to find some spot beneath it. A few were foolish enough not to allow for the tide and in due course, since the rain persisted all day, found themselves obliged to look for shelter elsewhere, all the covered space being packed to absolute capacity already. If the special train had been shunted into an unused bay at a terminal station it was known for a sympathetic station master to relieve their boredom and dejection by permitting them to board a couple of hours before the scheduled time of departure.

When the Clerk of the Weather smiled on them, as my father put it, the day lived up to all expectations, sand castles waiting to be built, a Punch and Judy show every so often, donkeys waiting for custom, fishermen with their rowing boats and even a couple of motor launches offering a "Trip Around the Bay" for 1/6d, which was often my choice if the pocket money would run to it after an ice cream cone, a twopenny plate of cockles or a pennyworth of winkles wrapped in newspaper, all of which I enjoyed with relish.

Because I'd saved so carefully—the Great Western even had its own bank in London Street immediately opposite the long drab 'Mess Rooms', deducting savings from wages if employees so wished—this particular year I decided I would persuade my mother to have a week's holiday at the seaside, and as soon as the notices appeared I approached her about it.

"It would be nice Hugh," she admitted with her kind smile, "but we can't really afford it. I'm not complaining, but Jane's not bringing anything in now she's apprenticed to millinery. I know your money helps, but it's your father's short time."

"I've thought of all that Mam," I assured her, "but you need a good break, someone to look after you for a week instead." I'd been watching her more closely than the others for some while, and was growing more concerned about her health. "I'm not only going to pay for myself, but paying for you as well."

"Oh no," she replied quickly, as I knew she would. "I wouldn't allow that. You've been working hard at something you don't like and I wouldn't dream of such a thing."

"Listen to me Mam. You've worked hard for us too, all these long years, even taking in all that washing, and I want you to have just one week free of everything except planning our food. What a nice time it would be for you, and we'd all be happy too."

"Well, you better see what your father says," partly conceded mother, "though it will be me who'll have to find the extra money."

"Not all of it!" I put in. "I intend to pay more than my share mind."

"I consider myself lucky to have such a good son as you," she said, giving me a rare hug.

"And I'm very lucky to have a mother just like you," I replied into her shoulder.

So addresses for 'rooms and attendance' in Paignton were sought from neighbours, a safer bet than taking them from the pages of *Holiday Haunts*, and eventually two bedrooms and a   81 dining room were booked with a Mrs. Webber about half a mile's walk from the sea for the four of us, Jane deciding to stay at home because her fiancé was planning a holiday for them later.

The big event seemed slower in coming than usual that year, though the last week scurried by for my mother with all the essential preparations to be accomplished, not only the washing and ironing and packing, but trying to work out a scheme of suitable meals to save the worry later; and of course ensuring father went to the Mechanics Institute at the correct time to pick up the family ticket and timetable of special trains. The latter required some understanding because you had to pick out your own train from a list of several going to diverse destinations. Of course I qualified for my own ticket and felt somewhat grown up as a consequence.

This holiday was almost as exciting to me as in the years of my boyhood, for the four of us were leaving home together for a whole week for the first time in years. It meant being up, as before, in the early hours to prepare food and drink for the journey and setting off with our luggage for the Dean Street entrance just the other side of the grim Rodbourne Bridges.

There were several lines of carriages at the sidings but I knew our train number and soon found it. It was an accepted principle that the middle of any train was the safest—in case of accident—as well as the smoothest, so I chose the sixth coach in the line and called for one of the workmen on duty to bring his steps which he did readily, sliding our cases in himself and assisting us up perhaps in the faint hope of earning a small tip. Later on, when there was much less room available, this became almost a necessity if you wanted him to find a place for you. As we had set out so early there was plenty of time to relax, and this became the longest forty minutes of the holiday before the quiet jolt told us our engine was being attached.

Promptly at 4.55 we drew away onto the main line and past the A Shop, partly obscured by the long line of 'dead' locomotives waiting their turn for repair, moving more briskly as the late G. J. Churchward's tall red brick house slipped by on the other side, then gathering speed towards Hay Lane, where the main line terminated for a while during construction, and were soon rushing through Wootton Bassett Station and on down Dauntsey

Bank. There was no need to speculate on the weather today for we were staying for the week once again, and left our fellow travellers in no doubt of the fact when the opportunity arose.

There were no hold-ups along the line and we slid into Paignton very close to time—a tribute to the planners—and having studied a street map of the town I soon led the family to our lodgings. The street was some way back from the town and because of the gradual rise we had to wait a few times for my mother to get her breath back. She was quite anaemic in those days and any extra exertion quickly tired her.

Our home for the following week proved to be a presentable terraced house, but a formal inspection of rooms was still the customary procedure and, in spite of the effort it demanded, my mother was shown around upstairs and finally emerged to say it was just as she'd hoped, clean, tidy, neat, if not exceptionally spacious. Mrs. Webber, a tall homely type in her early middle age greeted us all with a friendly smile and set about making a welcome cup of tea.

It was another couple of hours before we were ready for the promenade but mother persuaded us three to go without her as she preferred to rest and regain her strength after the tiring journey. Standing at the rails savouring the refreshing sea air we watched, almost unbelievingly, the sunshine dancing on the rippling water, while the gentle waves quenched themselves in the golden sands; below us the beach was already evenly covered with holiday makers including the large contingent of Swindon Day Trippers.

I was determined that the week's arrangements should hinge round my mother and to that end planned little trips when she felt inclined to go. Probably the most successful was the visit across the bay to Babbacombe, when the sea was wonderfully calm with only the merest breeze ruffling the surface and my mother sitting back completely relaxed and enjoying the scenery, first the residences of Torquay looking down proudly on its pier and harbour and then, after rounding the promontory, the lovely downs rising up some 300 feet above attractive Anstey's Cove, then Babbacombe and Oddicombe.

I also persuaded mother to look around the old world village of Cockington with its cottages of thatched roofs and leaded   83 windows; she sat down on one of the seats with Vera while father and I went off to find the centuries-old forge. I planned visits to Brixham and Torquay, but mother said they would be too hilly for her anyway and she would be happy enough sitting on the sands taking in the sea breezes alone, if need be, because she didn't want to spoil our pleasure. Once as we were ambling along the prom all together a photographer appeared from nowhere and clicked his camera quickly, which was just as well because my mother was never keen on having her photo taken. It proved to be a happy spontaneous group with me walking proudly alongside my mother with father and Vera on the other side, all in step, a unique memento I was to treasure for years to come.

Though at first we enjoyed Paignton front, once we found Goodrington Sands was less crowded we invariably made our way to its long stretch of clean beach, Vera and I paddling or swimming while mother and dad lazed in the sun in the luxury of deck chairs.

The week passed all too quickly, though my mother felt uneasy at times with so little to do. Our return 'special' was nothing like so crowded as on the outward journey, and coming back through the Somerset countryside my mother pointed out to me where she was born. Later, soon after passing through Castle Cary, she gripped my hand and said: "I'm glad you persuaded me to come Hugh. It's been a lovely time. Thank you my dear." To me, that was the perfect finish to one of the happiest weeks I could remember.

Yet another great annual social event was organised by the committee of the Mechanics Institute, the Children's Fête, a fitting climax to their summer holiday before returning to school. It was held early in August in the Park and preparations were put in hand a week before when a huge stage would be erected in one corner for first class circus artistes and others to entertain the crowds; then, nearer the day, the travelling showmen arrived to set out their grand amusements and stalls, making it the largest fair of its kind held anywhere in the West.

Promptly at 1.30 the gates opened and the children paid 2d to enter and were handed a half pound slab of wrapped fruit cake; also inside the bag was a ticket for a free ride on the roundabouts. The music from the organs and loud-speakers mingling with the throb of the steam engines could be heard well beyond the confines of the Park which, on the fine days everyone hoped for, would be crowded with thousands of adults and children from miles around.

Then at night would come the magnificent firework display, initiated by inflating a huge hot-air balloon which on release rose steeply into the gathering dusk and sailed away invariably towards the Continent. The ensuing spectacular display of cascades, naval battles, frolicking clowns, soaring rockets exploding into luminous stars, some topical event or personality all in fireworks, usually culminated in a realistic likeness of Their Majesties with the words: "God Save Our King" beneath; then parents and the children on their shoulders knew it was time to be making their way home. Even so, for those adults who still wanted more, a dance was arranged in the large Drill Hall alongside.

As I left my schooldays behind the Children's Fête lost some of its immense appeal, but like most other teenagers I never failed to be there, mixing with the joyous thronging crowds and partaking of some of its less venturesome attractions.

Reorganisation and its consequences 10

Fundamental changes were about to take place in the extension of the A Erecting Shop in the mid '30s. First of all the long-serving Foreman in the mould of G. J. Churchward, respected by all the men for his directness and fairness, was about to retire.

His second in command was likewise popular because of his pleasant manner and casual, almost carefree approach. He would stand and talk easily with his workers, perhaps even crack a genuine light joke or two, and had rarely been known to send a man out for a misdemeanour. He didn't favour the popular navy-blue but always dressed in tweeds and of course the distinguishing bowler hat, walked with a steady upright gait, and if he noticed you doing something contrary to the rules would stand up and stare until you became aware of him and desisted or you marched quickly on. He merely required, therefore, that his position should be respected, and this the vast majority acknowledged and reacted accordingly.

There was a third Foreman, a younger man in a different mould. He was quick and enthusiastic and moved around the immense workshop with a sense of purpose, alert and humourless. In his earlier days of promotion many workmen, apparently, looked upon him as a 'nine days wonder' because of his intense, impersonal manner and somewhat brief mode of speech.

"Give him three months and we'll cut him down to size, same as the rest," prophesied some of the more recalcitrant fitters. But after even three years this young Foreman showed no inclination to be cut down to size by any inferiors, nor of modifying his brisk style, I learnt, and as a result the detached amusement of a number of workers under him hardened into a sullen cynicism.

With only a few weeks to go before the Head Foreman's retirement it seemed a foregone conclusion that his second in command would step into the vacant shoes to everyone's peace of mind, but nothing was confirmed until the remaining few days. 87

King George V *outside A Shop*

The elder Foreman, favourite of the men without exception was turned down in favour of his younger and much less experienced inferior. The news as always spread around the workshop like a brushwood fire in drought, and with devastating effect. Could the management really be so out of touch with everyday affairs, the fitters asked one another. Sympathy was felt for their smitten and disgruntled favourite with consequent resentment being levelled at the enterprising aspirant, sentiments which were to sour workshop relations for some while to come.

Meanwhile two innovations unique in locomotive construction and repair in Britain were taking shape in the Extension. The first of these involved checking the alignment of engine frames, that is ensuring the axle-box guides were exactly true to the centre-line of the cylinders. Previously I had watched this being done many times by setting up a long thin cord through the centre of the cylinders as far as the rear axle-box guide, known as the hornblocks. Measurements for alignment were taken from this datum line to the other hornblocks as well. To complete the operation opposite hornblocks each side of the frame would be checked to ensure a true right angle with the long reference line, and if this was not registered the hornblocks must be ground down to achieve this, a laborious procedure I watched with interest whenever I could.

To speed up this process and ensure much greater accuracy an optical arrangement using a self-centering telescope within the cylinder and graduated brackets fixed along the locomotive frame with length bars was introduced, a design, I saw on the equipment, of the German firm of Carl Zeiss. Expert fitters were singled out for this intricate work and by their general attitude it was obvious even to me they were fully aware of their importance, now that the old traditional method of lining up with string, centre-pop and trammels was obsolete. The whole object of such precision, I also shortly learned, was that the more exact this alignment could be the more efficient would be the locomotive, and the longer it should run between repairs. 5023 *Brecon Castle* was the first to be built under the system and evidently, in time, all expectations were justified.

The second requirement was to improve on the tedious machining of the hornblocks, sometimes done by filing or more usually by means of small pneumatic hand-grinders, and this was now achieved by the installation of two sturdy grinding machines with arms swivelling up and down, and capable of moving horizontally on their long fixed beds.

The introduction of these devices produced considerable resentment amongst the men since it meant an appreciable saving of labour apart from other considerations, for such installations at the southern end of the workshop meant the loss of engine pits and a re-allocation of the remainder between the Chargemen.

This was the opportunity, or so the men believed, for the new Head Foreman to change completely the system of locomotive repairs in the Extension. Up to that time the locos awaiting repair were designated to one of the several gangs under its Chargeman, each gang being sited at three or four pits where the engine would be stripped completely down for a general repair (there were also intermediate repairs) and its frame checked and overhauled. The boiler was despatched for repair and all the other various parts were sent for cleaning in a caustic bosh, then sent to the other workshops for repairs, machining or renewal.

As they returned the components were re-assembled, the overhauled or replaced boiler installed, the locomotive wheeled, finished off almost as new and eventually put on trial. Other squads would also be involved of course, such as the valve-setters, platers, riveters, coppersmiths and painters, but the Chargeman to whom the engine was first assigned was in overall control.

Under the new proposed system the Extension was to be divided into four main sections, the first for stripping down as above. The second would be involved in work on the frames, examination by the Zeiss equipment, relining of cylinders and so on, and the grinding of hornblocks by the special machines. The third section would begin the basic assembly until the frame, complete with its boiler, could be put on its main wheels with coupling rods added. Since it was now mobile the locomotive would be moved by means of the traversing table running the length of the Extension to the other side, where the final assembly of pistons, valves, crossheads, connecting rods and the rest would take place.

I was intrigued by all this, including the strong opposition to this last major development. Union meetings were held in the 89 traversing bay at which the Communist Shop Steward was most vociferous in stating that these profound changes must be resisted at all cost, pointing out that one gang was going to be saddled with all the grease and filth with never any relief from it—the Stripping Gang. Others would become narrow specialists on repetitive work of the "utmost monotony", again with no prospect of experiencing the pride of seeing the job through to the end; and he forecast there would inevitably be a cut in all piecework rates and the balance the men took home every fortnight. On these grounds alone the changes must be opposed and seen for what they were, an attempt by the bosses to clamp down on the workers still more. By a show of hands the majority favoured his views, so he and his Committee went off to see the Head Foreman and put the matter "squarely in his court".

Most other tradesman in the AE were not involved in all this but, like myself, took a lively interest in all that was going on, especially when we learned the Head Foreman had proved adamant and would not concede an inch of ground. The present method, he insisted, was wasteful, men on each gang often hanging around for components from the machine shops, and the time to make some attempt to modernise the workshop was long overdue. Furthermore, to be fair to all, the four new gangs would receive the same piecework; the whole Shop would be pooled!

The Shop Steward and Committee were completely taken aback by such intransigence, even more so by that last stipulation; so they reported back that an impasse had been reached and the only resort was an all-out strike by every A.E.U. member. Yet bearing in mind the weeks of strike the boilermakers had endured years previously to get their extra shilling a week, there was a strong element of restraint from the rank and file at the mass meeting in the Traversing Bay, in spite of dire warnings in masterly oratory from the platform. Finally it was grudgingly accepted by a fair majority that the system be no longer opposed, provided assurances were given that earnings would not in any way suffer.

"But how can you bank on assurances given by a man like him?" demanded one outspoken fitter. He had nursed a personal grudge from the outset and indulged in a campaign of trying to poison the minds of his workmates. "We just can't trust the man! What's more once we accept there's no going back. We all lose out! Brothers, I propose we put it to the meeting again!" He was ruled "out of order".

It was unfortunate so much disfavour descended on the go-ahead overseer, for the men failed to realise at the time that all these developments were in essence the brainchild of the very energetic and far-seeing Works Manager, their Head Foreman being the subtly chosen instrument for putting it all more or less into effect; thus taking the resulting resentment, bitterness and aggression upon himself. The scheme went ahead in due course, though a last obstacle seemed to be getting some men to condemn themselves indefinitely to the undemanding and loathsome labour of the most detested job of all, the stripping down.

Even this was overcome by the shrewd Head Foreman, who persuaded a few particular fitters who'd never really made the grade and always been allocated the least responsible jobs on their own gangs, to take on the stripping down with an extra allowance for 'dirt money'. These men, well known for their limited ability, knew they would not be stretched in merely pulling a locomotive apart and the bonus, modest though it was, clinched the matter to their satisfaction.

The final stipulation that piecework earnings—the balance—must be pooled throughout the Extension, was something the men could hardly object to in the name of brotherhood and "equal shares for all", and though there were teething troubles for many months, when the scheme was firmly established with reviewed piecework rates the majority realised they were no worse off, and some of the original poorer gangs with less efficient Chargehands were distinctly better off.

Further, though grudgingly accepted, it became patent to all but the most prejudiced that the circuit method of repairs was much more efficient, with the locomotives coming in at the end of one long row of pits and emerging completed at the end of the opposite row. Yet the antagonism towards the man deemed responsible for the metamorphosis lingered on.

It erupted again in the spring of 1935 when, to celebrate its centenary, the Great Western Railway inaugurated a new express, *The Bristolian*, covering the run from London to Bristol non-stop in 1¾ hours. Everyone in the AE Shop including myself was stirred by this and knew the express leaving Paddington at 10 a.m.

Arlington Grange, *September 1936*

would be thundering past the home of its birth at 11.06. So almost to a man we decided to down tools for ten minutes and line up outside the long workshop to wave the historic train on its way.

Excitement rose as the time approached, but imagine the frustration and indignation of everybody when with almost military precision a line of carriages was deliberately shunted in front of us almost as the familiar beat could be heard in the vicinity of the Junction Station less than a mile up the line. A few men, recklessly determined not to be outdone, scrambled beneath the coaches to the other side, just in time to see the express go roaring by with dignitaries and Directors actually standing up in the corridors and waving back an acknowledgement to the men who were making such things possible. Of course this was denied me and the countless others, and when it quickly became known the men's fury and renewed resentment of the man they felt had organised the manoeuvre erupted all over again. "We've got to let him know just what we feel," the ringleaders swore. "At dinner time we'll all drum him out!"

The message caught on with customary speed. Anything that would produce a din was brought to hand in preparation. I saw the antagonistic fitter, already mentioned, wheeling the brass bell of No. 6000 *King George V*, which happened to be in for repairs at the time, up towards the New Work in a sack truck, where he set it up jubilantly so that its tongue was free to swing.

At 12.25 an unearthly silence settled upon the whole workshop. Though the Foremen's office was actually in the AW Shop it could be clearly seen from the New Work Section, and soon the door opened and out stepped the Head Foreman, first as always. He paused, then moved briskly down the tall flight of stairs to disappear for a moment, hidden by machinery.

They waited until he was firmly on his own territory and began the long trek up the perimeter of the vast workshop. *King George's* bell shattered the tranquillity with a stark frightening clangour, a signal for bedlam to be let loose. Not all fitters took part, but many had a hammer in hand and found some means of joining in the bizarre orchestration, be it on a tin drum, a piece of iron, length of boiler tube or even a dismantled locomotive whistle. For one moment the Foreman was seen to pull up in his tracks, turn pale, then collect himself and resume his usual stride with head held high on that seemingly endless journey up the length of the Engine Shed, as it was sometimes called by those not working there.

Each engine bay added its contribution as he went by until it seemed the whole shop was in uproar. At long last, after probably the most harrowing walk of his life, he reached the east door, grabbed it open and slammed it angrily behind him, for the other two Foremen had lagged well in the rear, the tumult slowly dying like the ending of a storm as they made their leisurely way, the workmen endeavouring to make it obvious there was only one target for their bitter resentment.

After checking out that dinner time I could hardly wait to tell my father all about this incredible incident, but the Factory grapevine had done its work and he was already aware of the bare details.

"It was a terrible racket Dad," I assured him, anxious he should know it was first-hand knowledge. "Mind you," I added reflectively, "I felt sorry for him really, it was so overwhelming."

"Did you have any part in it?"

"Of course not Dad. But I admit I felt angry when those carriages deliberately blocked our view and we could only hear the rattle of *The Bristolian* as it rushed by. It was a silly thing to do."

"Be careful what you say," warned my father. "There might be some good reason why it was done, and p'raps somebody higher up gave the order. You never know with these things. Just always keep out of trouble. It never pays to stick your neck out."

"I'll remember what you say Dad. But I don't think I shall ever forget what happened today."

Neither did the men involved. But as soon as work resumed that afternoon the Chief Shop Steward was called to the Foremen's office and it apparently emerged that the trend of their conversation was something along these lines: "What is the meaning of such disgraceful behaviour Ferguson?"

"Well," replied the shop representative suavely, "you will know the men were a bit uptight about the way they were treated this morning."

"And do you endorse such blatant insubordination? Do you?" 95

"I can't say I do. But neither do I endorse the rather obvious attempt to nullify the men's spontaneous enthusiasm."

"I didn't ask that! You do seem to condone their action, then?"

It should be said that Ferguson was a shrewd, fearless character whose ardent political beliefs coloured all his dealings with capitalist employers and officials.

"I've already told you, I don't endorse it. For your information I played no part in the whole affair, not the flag-waving, as it were, nor the men's reaction to that rather silly cover up. You appreciate the fact that some of the men who got under the coaches at the risk of their lives, I may say, actually saw your Directors standing up and waving back at them. That was the last straw."

"I'm more concerned with the most humiliating thing that has ever happened to any Foreman in these works. And you could have prevented it if you wished."

"By the size of the demonstration you must realise the matter was completely out of my hands. I repeat I had nothing whatever to do with it."

"You're a very clever person Ferguson. I demand to know who the instigators were, so that they can be suitably dealt with."

"I really don't know. And if I did, would you really expect me to tell you? It would be more than my position is worth. I'm in this to serve the men, not betray them. It was one of those things. It just blew up."

"You are also paid by the Company Ferguson, don't forget that! Since you refuse me the names of the culprits, I demand a written apology for the appalling incident from your Shop Committee and on behalf of all the men."

Ferguson apparently gave the request a few moments of thought.

"We are a democratic organisation you know. I can give you no such assurance at this stage. But I will pass on your demand when the Committee next meets, though it is only fair to say I'm not very optimistic about the chances."

"Failing that," put in the Foreman incisively, "I will have to consider what other steps must be taken to ensure there is no repetition of such riotous behaviour. I expect that apology within the next couple of days. That will be all."

The Shop Steward turned to the door, but just before he reached it the Foreman spoke again: "I think I have a good idea of at least one person who's behind all this."

The Shop Steward turned to him quickly.

"Really? Then don't you think it would be a sounder idea to name him and produce some evidence to substantiate your suspicions?"

"Perhaps in good time, Ferguson. Perhaps all in good time."

But no apology was forthcoming. The Shop Steward, who had his eyes on promotion within the Union (to the post of full-time Organiser, which he eventually attained) knew it would strengthen his claim if he capitalised on the situation. He called his Shop Committee for a short briefing and recommended them to refer the matter to the next Branch meeting. Here, when detailing the interview at great length he emphasised the threats of the Foreman to the utmost, stressing how he "stood up fearlessly" to the aggrieved Head Foreman and would not concede "one iota".

"I therefore propose brothers," he apparently concluded, "we reject this man's demands categorically, and proceed as if the matter is closed". It was seconded, put to the meeting and carried unanimously.

Some while after this a major confrontation between the management and the boilermakers seemed to be looming. I was led to understand that for nearly 25 years the men of my trade had been smouldering under the ignominy of having a fitter as their Head Foreman as mentioned earlier, chosen by the C.M.E. at the time as a move "to bring precision into boiler manufacture", itself almost insulting and quite provocative to hard-working independent men. Had the Foreman not treated all boilermakers with such condescension they might have tolerated him a little more kindly. As it was they looked upon him as a very unpleasant person to say the least, and there was tremendous relief when his retirement was mooted which was coupled with a determination by all boilermakers that never again would they be subjected to supervision from anyone other than one of their own trade.

To this end the District Organiser of the Union at Southampton was briefed and great emphasis placed on the volatile situation that would result if the men's wishes were not 97 put into effect. In due course that official arrived in Swindon, addressed the men at a special meeting, then sought an audience with the Works Manager, who had only been appointed two months earlier. While not given a positive assurance in the matter, he came away sufficiently confident that the men's feelings would be borne firmly in mind when the appointment was to be made a few weeks later.

His judgement was justified and the men's anxiety appeased in due course when the second in command in the Boiler Shop was moved up and this trend established. Everyone in the Shop was now content over the issue, for their new superior was a complete contrast, a pleasant, understanding and conciliatory individual prepared to judge a workman on his merits, and had only a few more years to go before retiring himself. It so happened he was a distant relative of our family, a third cousin of my father in fact, but we never made contact, and I kept the relationship to myself throughout my apprenticeship.

Tragedy strikes home

11

For the next few weeks things seemed to be more rational in the AE Shop. The Head Foreman certainly appeared somewhat affected by all that had happened and there was the obvious rumour that he'd contemplated resigning his position, though this was more likely wishful thinking on the part of the small band who might never be reconciled to working loyally under him. The sober majority, however, felt they might have over-reacted by such blatant action and were willing to give their overseer a chance to redeem himself.

At least such incidents as this certainly broke the depressing monotony of the job for me. I now hated the sight of rivets, the acrid fumes from the forge, the all-pervading dust in my hair and down my collar, the long frequent trek up the yard beyond the A Shop for the binful of fine coke, and the over-riding humility of being nothing more than a labourer when you were supposed to be learning a trade. I approached the Chargeman on several occasions about getting off rivet heating but each time I was told there was no hope for some while, which I guessed meant I was going to be stuck on the hateful job until I turned 18.

But often now while at work my mind sadly turned to a worrisome matter at home; my mother's weakening condition. She had been pale as long as I could remember—her complexion almost white, like porcelain in fact—but now she was becoming distressingly breathless. She found our stairs too steep and on many occasions I had seen her stop halfway with the slop pail, which she always kept discreetly covered, to regain her breath; now it was every three stairs. If I offered to carry it up and down for her she stoutly refused, saying it was not a boy's job.

The G.W.R. Medical Fund Society, to give it the full title, functioned in a large specially designed brick building on the corner of Milton Road, consisting of several surgeries for doctors, a huge dispensary, offices, and on the upper floor a dental surgery. The other half of the building was taken up by two 99 swimming baths, a large and small one, and in the winter the former was boarded over and used as a dance hall-cum-entertainments centre, where outstanding performers might also be engaged to appear.

I well remember my father, being musically inclined, speak of the coming of the famous soprano Dame Clara Butt, and how he would love to hear her inspiring voice. Naturally he couldn't afford even the cheapest seat, but not to be outdone, went along on the night standing as near as he could to one of the side doors and listening enraptured as the powerful, moving voice echoed from the high roof almost as clearly to those outside, who applauded just as enthusiastically as the privileged ones within. Father was so impressed he decided to wait behind and catch a glimpse of the *prima donna* when she eventually left so that he could say he'd not only heard her in reality, but seen her too. He did just get a glimpse of her smile as she acknowledged the cheers before descending the steps of the main entrance to enter her limousine. He talked of it for days afterwards.

Each of the consulting rooms in the "Surgery", as the main building was called, bore on its door the name of the next doctor in attendance, each of these medical men on the staff being allocated an area of the town as his normal practice. There was never a shortage of doctors engaged by the Society for their salaries were adequate and assured, and since the Medical Fund was under the aegis of the G.W.R., other privileges were available not usually accorded to their profession.

If you wished to visit your doctor you must present your yellow membership book at the small office and be issued with a metal check bearing your consultation number, and this you placed in a box on the wall of the surgery as your turn came round. The little yellow book was in effect your family medical record, for the doctor would write relevant information on its pages, almost illegibly of course, and noted any necessary prescriptions. Then crossing to the large dispensary, one section of which was for 'Ladies Only', you stood in the queue until you reached the tiny pigeonhole, passed through the book and waited for the medicine to be made up; all in all a tedious proceeding, for the dispensers were the essence of tardiness.

Opposite the Surgery in Faringdon Road stood the Company

Estate, owned exclusively by the Railway and consisting of several streets of humble but solidly-built terraced cottages in Bath stone, built for the workers and their families when the Factory was first established.

In the same unassuming style and also of grey stone stood the Cottage Hospital, on the edge of the Estate and almost opposite the Surgery, having two small wards, an operating theatre and a casualty department at the rear, not too far from the main entrance to the Works for accident purposes; but in the late twenties the little hospital proved woefully inadequate and a temporary square asbestos annexe was erected on the lawn in front of the original building.

My mother had been under the doctor more or less for two or three years, but he was a gruff almost frightening man with chunky glasses who spoke abruptly with a lisp and often smelt of whisky. He was the old-fashioned physician who held little brief for surgery except in dire emergency, one reason for this it was said, being that he'd lost a favourite teenage daughter in the theatre undergoing an operation for appendicitis.

That being so, it became too much of an effort for my mother to visit him and each time he called he passed her off as anaemic and merely prescribed her another bottle of a well-known blood tonic, containing so much iron that it darkened her teeth. But as her condition gradually weakened so his interest waned, and to such an extent one of us would wait to see his car in the street and almost beg him to call on our mother. I knew there was something seriously wrong with her and this was confirmed one day when I caught a glimpse inside the slop pail and saw it contained a considerable amount of blood. I would lay awake at night worrying about her and trying to shake off the growing premonition that the outcome of it all would prove to be calamitous and perhaps even tragic.

One Wednesday afternoon I was brushing out the side tanks of a 4800 0-4-2 Tank—another chore I hated since it was not only dirty but confining too—when there was a bang on the side and a call for me to come out. I struggled backward to the daylight with the lighted candle in my hand, held my arms above my head to squeeze my upper body through the small manhole, believing someone was playing a prank, but found myself staring down at our tall Chargehand instead. "Come on out at once!" he ordered. "You're wanted home straight away!"

Knowing instinctively what was wrong I discarded my overalls hurriedly, stowed them away in the sack truck of tools, dashed across to the Boiler Bay to throw in my check and practically ran all the way up the main thoroughfare of the AM Shop. I hadn't stopped to think of a pass-out but the Watchman on the gate had already been notified and waved me through. Once out into the road I sped past the blank wall of the P1 shop and turned into Linslade Street to see my father trotting along ahead. I soon caught him up and we ran abreast for a while with scarcely a word between us.

"It's Mam, isn't it?" I asked when we were forced to slow down momentarily to catch our breath.

"'Fraid so . . . Don't sound . . . so good."

"She's been very ill for a long time, Dad. Something should've been done about it before."

"Ah, I just hope it ain't too late," said my father, and started to run again as best he could.

When we arrived indoors my sister greeted us with tears. Fortunately Wednesday was her half-day off and as usual she'd come straight home.

"She just collapsed and passed out on the bed, Dad," she explained between sobs. "It terrified me. I thought she was dead. I phoned for the special doctor." This was another aspect of the commendable medical system, a doctor being on call for emergencies 24 hours a day.

"I better go up an' see her," said my father, and crept quietly up the stairs in case of disturbing her. I followed.

My mother heard us and slowly opened her listless eyes. Her face was drawn and no longer white, but ashen.

"I'm sorry Harry," she said weakly. "But I can't go on . . . like this . . . any longer."

He touched her hand as it rested limply on the quilt, but dare not grip it because she bruised so very easily.

"Don't worry Mary," he tried to comfort her, doing his best to hide his real feelings. "We're goin' to see you all right now. It's gone on long enough."

102   Her lids slowly closed, and as he thought she might be going

off to sleep he stood silently at the side of the bed still lightly touching her hand which seemed so very cold. I got him a chair, and some minutes later there was a sharp rap on the knocker of the front door, and when my sister had briefed him the doctor came hurrying up the stairs. A glance and the briefest of examinations was all he needed.

"How long has she been like this?" he asked in astonishment.

"On and off for months," put in my sister quickly. "Almost years."

"Who is her doctor?" When told he merely grunted, then turned to my mother. "My dear," he said kindly, "you've been very ill. But we're going to get you into hospital immediately, so don't worry any more. You're going to be taken good care of."

Mother smiled her gratitude fleetingly, then drifted off again.

"I want wooden blocks about nine inches high to prop up the bottom of the bed, then she must not be disturbed until the ambulance comes."

I soon found what was wanted from the 'old timber' father kept stored in the yard and between us we did as the doctor instructed; then reassuring mother once again he left to make the necessary arrangements. The ambulance came inside twenty minutes, and having made provision for a neighbour to take care of my other sister when she arrived from school, the three of us were allowed to travel to the hospital since no attendant was provided in those days. My mother was admitted to the more modern annexe and we waited in the corridor until she was settled in, when a tall, slim and very smart nursing sister came along.

"How long has she been like this?" she likewise asked incredulously.

My sister repeated her answer to the doctor, and added: "But it's been getting worse for a long time."

"She should have been here months ago," was the anticipated reply. "Who was her doctor?"

When I spoke up she lifted her shoulders indignantly and let out an impatient sigh.

"Well, you must realise she is extremely ill, but we will do all we can for her. You may see her now for a few moments, and when the surgeon has examined her tomorrow he will want to speak to you."

We went back to the hospital to see him early the following evening.

"Your wife is in a very serious condition," he told father. "She requires an immediate operation but is far too weak to undergo it. We have to try and build her up until she is ready, but that in itself is going to take time. Even so the operation will be a very major one and could last from three to four hours. She should never have been allowed to go on so long."

"We know," put in my sister. "We've been trying to tell this to Dr. . . ."

"I fully understand," cut in the surgeon sharply. "It is her future we must work on now."

After a family conference it was decided my younger sister should stay for a few weeks at Hambrook with our favourite aunt and uncle, and at the first week-end went cheerfully away with father, in fact quite looking forward to the change in the hope it might mean an unexpected holiday—a break in her schooling— which unfortunately for her proved not to be the case.

On our first visit my mother was full of praise for the nurses.

"They are wonderful," she said. "I keep apologising for all the work I'm making them. So much washing. But all they say is: 'You mustn't worry. All we want is for you to get better.'"

Trip Week was approaching again and we'd previously decided on a day's visit to Teignmouth, but now considered we should call it off in the circumstances. My mother would have none of it.

"You go off and enjoy yourselves," she insisted. "You all owe it to yourselves. I shall be quite all right here."

We went, but our hearts weren't in the visit whatsoever. Time and again we found ourselves looking at each other in mutual thought, preoccupied with our frail one tucked away in the annexe so many miles distant, and what we would have sacrificed to have her with us.

We arrived at Swindon Junction around 1.30 next morning and since the way home was quite near the Hospital couldn't resist going to the daily bulletin board, striking matches in the almost complete darkness in attempts to read the surgeon's inevitable scrawl:

104   "Mrs. Freebury—Rather poorly"

This particular phrase was generally accepted as ominous and indicative of a gradual deterioration, more significant than "Seriously Ill" even.

All the more surprising that a few days later, at the next visiting time, we walked into the ward to find my mother sitting up in bed, looking so much brighter and sounding remarkably cheerful.

"I'm better than I've been for a long time," she greeted us. "I want to come home now."

"Oh Mam, you're not quite fit yet," Jane reminded her. "You must get a bit stronger first."

"No, I'm all right Jane. I'm really feeling fine. Please let me come home to you."

"Perhaps it would be rather unwise just now Mam," I put in gently. "They're all working so well for you it might undo a lot of good."

"Oh I so much want to come home and be with you all," she pleaded. "I promise I won't be any more trouble than I can help!"

"You're never any trouble Mam," put in Jane sweetly. "And you know just how much we love you. We only want what's best for you, that's all. Please trust us." Much of the remaining visiting time was spent in this vein, and as we walked away and waved from the end of the ward it was obvious she was dispirited and holding back her tears. It made us all feel guilty, but since with visiting times being so restricted we wouldn't be seeing her for three more days Jane wrote her a lovely letter saying some of the things we were planning to do when she was back with us.

But on the following Saturday, as soon as we stepped into the ward, we realised how false was that recovery and how hollow our hopes. She looked desperately ill, more than we'd ever seen her, and by her head was a kidney bowl into which she had vomited.

"Oh dear," she sighed in a quieter moment. "I can't make it. It's too much. I just can't bear any more Harry . . ."

My dad and I were so numbed we could only sit there mutely for a time, completely deflated. He held one of her white, near-fleshless hands, while I supported her head behind the pillow towards the bowl as she needed it.

"Don't give up Mam," I whispered to her as she lay back again. "You've done so well so far. We're all proud of you, you know."

The faintest smile relaxed her lips for a moment, then with lids still closed she shook her head lightly.

"It's no use Hugh," she said slowly. "It's just too late."

This was the most distressing visit of all, the longest we'd known, just sitting there watching a loved one suffering in pain. We greatly missed the support of my sister who worked all day on Saturdays at the shop, and when the bell rang for the termination of visiting, we left the ward so utterly despondent we walked home past the Park and under the Bridges in near silence and abject thought. We were almost as wordless preparing the tea, longing for my sister to join us, yet apprehensive about her reaction to our depressing news.

In the event, after an initial response that brought all three of us near to tears, she realised we needed her support as surely as she needed ours, and tried to be philosophical.

"You're always saying, Dad," she reminded him, "if only we have faith things will work out right in the end. So we can only pray and hope this is only temporary and she's going to pull through in the end."

"Ah, that's true," agreed my father. "If only we have enough faith! I don't know what I'd do without you children round me!"

We sat down at the table in no mood to eat, but needed the cup of tea. Then I told them I was going up to my small back bedroom. Once there I knelt down reverently and prayed as never before, prayed that my dearest mother would be spared, pointed to what a good life she'd always led, working so hard for us, never doing a soul any harm . . . and too young to die so soon . . . !

I was arrested in my intercession by an urgent bang on the front door, and when my sister answered I looked down the stairs and saw a little nurse in the porch, a raincoat over her uniform, breathless from having run all the way from the bus-stop.

"Will you come back at once please," she said jerkily. "She is now very much worse."

When we got to the Hospital we sat in the narrow corridor mutely and despondently until the Ward Sister eventually came along.

"I'm very much afraid things have taken a turn for the worse," she said gravely. "You may see her for a short while, but try not to distress her please."

106

She led us to a small private ward, and here we stood at the bedside waiting silently for some response from that pain-wracked figure who was once a radiant wife and loving mother. Presently the fragile lids slowly opened and the still blue eyes drifted in our direction.

"Hello," she said weakly. "I—I can't make it. It's all over . . . I'm sorry for all the trouble I've caused you . . ."

"You've been no trouble at all, Mam," my sister hastened to assure her. "You've been wonderful, and so brave."

"And Harry," my mother spoke quietly again in due course, "I'm sorry . . . sorry for the times we've fallen out . . . Try and understand."

"No, no! Please Mary!" sobbed my dad, touched to his depths. "I should be saying that. You've always been such a good wife to me, and devoted mother to the children."

She gave the hint of a thin smile.

"Go now," she said simply. "Don't worry about me. Make sure you take care of my baby." We nodded, knowing what she meant.

In turn we kissed her and filed out, to sit in the lonely corridor for perhaps half an hour; then a nurse came up to us again.

"She seems to have rallied a little," she told us, "and has asked to see you once more." But at the door the nurse pulled on my arm, holding me back. "Just those two first," she whispered.

For a moment I was bewildered, then understood. When my dad and sister emerged they were doing their best to look composed.

"Send in my boy," I heard my mother say. With that I could wait no longer, but rushed in, dropped on my knees at the side of the bed, and buried my face in her moist but still soft and lovely fair hair, her cheek moving slightly in contact with me.

"Oh Mam . . . Mam!" I cried. "Please don't leave us! We all need you so much!"

"There, there," she comforted me weakly, patting the back of my head. "Don't be so upset. And don't pine for me. You've been a good boy. Now be brave for your dad and the others. She held my head lovingly for a little longer, then whispered: "Kiss me goodbye, Hugh."

I did so, and rose from her with tears rolling down my cheek.

"I'll never forget you," I promised her. "I shall love you 107 always." With one last look, ashamed of my unbridled emotion, I stumbled out to join the others.

Soon after 8 p.m. the Day Sister came along on her way off duty.

"I'm terribly sorry," she said with feeling. "She's been such a marvellous patient. Not a single word of complaint ever came from her lips. She was brought here just too late. Do forgive me." She turned abruptly to hide her sadness, then strode briskly down the corridor.

Two junior nurses soon followed, came to my sister and, eyes brimming with tears, kissed her in turn.

"She was so wonderful," one said brokenly. The other nodded, then they also hurried away with heads bowed.

In due course the Night Sister invited the three of us into a small sitting-room. We tried to relax in the deep arm chairs, each numbed and withdrawn in anguish, and even when darkness crept in, sleep would not come. Yet at some stage we must have dozed off for we were disturbed by the soft insistent voice of the Sister.

"It is all over now," she said simply. "Perhaps you would just like to have a last look at her."

My dear mother was buried in the large cemetery at Whitworth Road. Before she was taken from our home for the last time, her father gazed down at the features that were once such a pleasure to behold; and he wept. She was the only daughter of his first marriage, and he might never know how cruelly she was treated in her early years by a jealous stepmother, making her little more than a servant to the six children who came after her, yet to whom my mother bore no resentment for the favouritism they all received, except the eldest, at her expense.

"If only I'd known," my grandfather cried unashamedly as I stood at his side. "Money would've been no object."

Of course you knew, I thought rather scornfully. She was in hospital for four weeks and we wrote from the start telling you how ill she was. Yet neither you nor grandmother, only 35 miles away, bothered to come and see her. We know how you helped your other children, even after they married, but because my mother was too proud to ask, you never saw our need; nor really cared very much about your three eldest grandchildren.

I moved away, feeling quite detached from him. Then I realised this was something my mother would never wish! So instead, I turned back to comfort him in his genuine distress, and escorted him from our small front room when he was sufficiently composed to return to the others. Only later did I learn that as he gazed on her it brought back vivid memories of her own mother, his first wife, who had died at an even earlier age.

The Company Dispensary

Reflections

12

For a time our family withdrew within itself, gaining some measure of comfort, individually, from the knowledge that our great loss was equally shared and each of us must try and support the others. My younger sister was not quite of the age to appreciate fully the wide gulf that was to exist in our home for months to come, while having been absent for those few crucial and dispiriting weeks had softened the blow of feeling motherless to some extent. That of course had been another, unspoken, reason for deciding to send her to relations; now we others remembered the pledge to her mother and consequently for a while at least perhaps indulged her a little more than we should.

Meanwhile my elder sister immediately volunteered to give up her job, though she would have been a qualified milliner within a few months, and was willing to accept the responsibilities of running the home provided some basic alterations and adjustments were made to our way of life. Firstly, the old-fashioned cast-iron fireplace with its hob on one side and cracked oven on the other surmounted by the tall mantelpiece must go, just as soon as the landlord could be persuaded to replace it with a more up-to-date and presentable item requiring far less work to keep clean.

"You realise the rent is so low we don't make a penny out of the place," said Mr. Grey when first approached, a remark always tendered when repairs requiring urgent attention were brought to his notice. But my sister pressurised father to insist and eventually the compromise was reached that the rent should be raised 3d a week to allay the cost. Next, with the departure of the old black grate with its high fender and elaborate fire-irons (a wedding present which my mother had assiduously polished with Brasso every Saturday morning) a secondhand gas stove was an essential for the back kitchen. This and other things were not achieved overnight, but my eighteenth birthday was coming along when I would qualify for that "big rise" amounting to

111

Train to catch! 1934

something like 7/6d basic a week, and naturally I would contribute much more for my keep to help things along.

Because of the deep affection between us I took the loss of my mother profoundly to heart, hiding my grief from the others as much as possible. Though neither of my parents were ardent churchgoers they attended occasionally until my mother's health began to fail, and took some interest in parochial affairs. Further they insisted that all three of us children regularly supported the Sunday school in Rodbourne Lane, called the Mission Hall, as well as the tall red-brick church at the end of our street of which it was a part. Sometimes on a winter's evening all the family would gather round the glowing fire, singing hymns each chose in turn, while unfailingly every night since a small boy I said my prayers before getting into bed, and long before my mother was rushed to hospital I was always asking earnestly for her return to normal health. Those weeks she was away from us I had pleaded more devoutly than ever, but all to no avail.

Now I was in the throes of a reaction, my mind slipping back bitterly to those frequent Friday dinner times when, although warned the "balance" would be right down again, my father's pay tin held even less than expected. My Dad would wait till the meal was over and he was ready to return to the Factory.

"Well Mary," he would say, "I'm afraid it's not very much again. It's all the blessed stoppages what do it. Four hundred of coal this week, as well as the wood and the Medical Fund. Sorry I can't make it any more. See you tonight."

He would put his meagre contribution on the table beside her and move away as if he was already late, relieved to get it over at last. My mother would stare absently at the couple of notes and a few silver coins, and wait until the outside door had closed behind him.

"What's the good of that to me?" she would sob to no one in particular. "How can I do anything with it? The bills are already piling up. There's the rent to come out of it, two lots of grocery—I owe for last week as well, and the baker's bill to be settled up in a fortnight. I can't do it. I just can't do it!"

It was a rule of the Co-operative Bakery Society that while credit was allowed to a tolerable amount, outstanding bills must be paid up at each half year's ending. More than once my father had to seek an interview with the Secretary to plead for an extension, and if this was not forthcoming to consider approaching someone on his gang in the AM Shop for a loan, one of them a bookie's runner—he would have been instantly sacked if caught—who boasted he had a "nice little bit put to one side".

My father's basic rate of 40/- a week was augmented by a War Bonus of 16/6d, being a legacy of the Great War to keep up with the cost of living. But piecework was calculated only on the basic rate so that a 10% Balance (common enough for the poorly-run Axlebox Gang) amounted to 4/- for the fortnight. Furthermore this was for the 47 hour week, which had not been worked for several years. In fact I could remember when the Factory was open only four days a week, one day more than would have allowed the workers to qualify for the dole if they survived the Means Test, but following a recovery only Saturday mornings were dropped.

Then I thought of all the washing my mother did in a desperate effort to balance the weekly budget, not just for the five of us, but the large bundle for Mrs. Watkins dumped in the porch each Monday morning, and Tuesday's chore of going down the street to Mrs. Wainwright, Eddie's mother, and staying much of the day to scrub her family wash, clean up and even start her ironing on a drying day; and all for 1/6d! It just didn't make sense, and many a time we told her it amounted to near slavery and she should either charge more or give up the soul-destroying drudgery altogether. But she would simply say: "I know it's hard work, but we've been friends for a long time, and I don't feel like saying anything now."

Why could she not have been spared to enjoy the fruits of those seemingly endless labours? Only a few months more would have seen the beginning of brighter days. I would have been adding considerably to the family budget from increased earnings, while my elder sister would have completed her apprenticeship and qualified as a milliner and window-dresser with something resembling a salary in return; soon also my other sister would be 14, and was already determined to leave school at Christmas to add further to the incomings.

Such unhappy and depressing reflections naturally turned me against my job more than ever, and a burning conviction took root that I was wasting my life with this interminable trekking to and 113 fro twice every day, merely an insignificant and expendable item, plodding stoically along with those thousands of others at the behest of the wailing hooter, only to be swallowed up in that massive all-absorbing complex week in and month out.

The desire to do something eminently more useful with my life was kindled within me afresh, something whereby I could possibly render service to others, perhaps in the medical line in some hospital or other, perhaps with the remote chance of becoming a teacher. But of course I was hampered by having no worthwhile paper qualifications so far to commend me, other than the pleasing school-leaving report of which my mother had been so inordinately proud. I was completely hamstrung, pinned down with not the vaguest hope in any direction other than that which Fate had inexorably ordained for me.

The only flicker at the end of the grim tunnel was the certainty I would be leaving rivet-hotting behind me within the next few weeks.

Interesting work at last

13

Unfortunately even this belief proved to be something of a misapprehension, for on the Friday prior to my eighteenth birthday the Chargeman sought me out with these words: "On Monday I want you to start work on the cab jigs over in the Boiler Bay."

My hopes were flattened yet again though it shouldn't have come as much of surprise, since I'd noticed the holder-up engaged there eyeing me up on more than one occasion, and had actually overheard him asking Larry Carter what kind of a boy I was.

It meant I was to be consigned to the two jigs on which new engine cabs were assembled and the work involved, as far as I was concerned, was riveting pure and simple. If the holder-up who was in charge, in practice if not in theory, had been any other the work might have been tolerable for a short while. As it was I knew I would be unable to take to this particular man whose attitude and values were alien to the way I had been brought up. Yet I suppose in the final analysis he was a rather sad figure and basically very unsure of himself.

The accepted routine on the cab-work stint was that if the holder-up took to you there was every likelihood you would be stuck with him for a year or more, only to finish up stay-bashing or hand riveting on the loco boilers because you were "well broken in"; so I resolved this wasn't going to be my lot for long. I reported for duty as requested and was shown how to heat the small rivets on the perforated plate resting on the fire, pass them to the holder-up outside the cab who, after placing the rivet in the hole, would cover the round head with his snap dolly for the other apprentice in the squad to hammer down from the inside. It was understood the riveting was shared equally by the two apprentices, but it was well over a week before I was allowed my first chance with the hammer.

Much of the work obviously involved knocking down rivets in tight corners, at which I proved not to be very accomplished, 115 frequently catching the hammer on some projection or other and missing the early strokes by which time the rivet had cooled and had to be withdrawn. If this happened too often it annoyed the holder-up, who would shout from the other side: "For God's sake hit the bloody thing first time, why can't you!"

I was not unduly perturbed, even knowing my bungling efforts would most likely be going back to the Foreman, for it was part of my plan; and when it came to the cold riveting of the beading round the edges of the cab I genuinely couldn't cope. The rivets might be $1/8$in. or $3/16$in. diameter, and first they must be roughed over then neatly rounded off with a sharp little snap tool. But if the nobble was in the slightest too flat, the snap would cut into the metal plate all round, invoking the sharp displeasure of the Foreman when he happened to catch sight of it.

For in the Boiler Bay you were too often and too closely under the shrewd surveillance of that gentleman for my liking, though this didn't deter the odd workman from making game of the innocent lads coming straight into the Shop from school. If one of them didn't appear too bright in catching on to the work he might be told in irritation: "Go and see the bloke in the Stores. Tell 'im Charlie said you want a very long stay. And don't be long." If the obliging youth queried what length was required, the answer might well come back: "Just as long as 'e likes."

The lad would present himself at the hatch of the Stores under the Foreman's office and state his request. Provided he was not too busy, with a twinkle in his eye the Storekeeper might say: "Well, it'll take a bit o' time, so stand there at one side." The youth might wait patiently for five minutes before asking again if he could have the stay.

"It ain't quite long enough yet," might be the retort, and the Storeman would disappear again behind his racks until wanted by someone else. When he could see the puzzled youngster getting agitated he would lean on the metal shelf of the door and dismiss him with: "Tell Charlie I hope it was long enough!"

Another request to a simple tyro might be to get a bucket of wind for the pneumatic hammer. If the Storeman was busy or not in the best of moods some very coarse language could ensue; otherwise he might say: "Ain't you got a lid for the bucket? Won't keep in without it." Back the innocent lad would trek to the amusement of his tormentors. Further requests could be for a left-handed hammer, or a broom to be re-bristled, in which case the rejoinder would be: "Tell 'im I've run out o' bristles."

I was lucky in not once being the victim of such pranks coming into the workshops at 16 rather than direct from school, and hearing about such things as office boy I was on my guard anyway.

During that month I learnt very little, other than by watching Sid Matthews building up the next cab on the nearby jig, nor was I frightened to ask him questions, which the Leading Hand seemed flattered to answer. One day after fixing the roof to a cab he called me over.

"Don't let on I said anything mind," he cautioned me, "but I reckon you're wasting your bloody time on this job. Take a tip from me and get a move back on the new work."

"Thank you," I replied politely. "I would like to very much. But how do I go about it?"

"As far as I see you're doing all right in that direction," returned the plater wryly. "Keep it up and it won't be long."

Whether he brought any pressure to bear I was never to know, but a week later the Chargeman presented himself again.

"I'm giving you another move," he said, "and I don't want you to let me down this time. Come with me."

Yes, I was off back to the A Extension where the new work was becoming quite interesting! I was taken along to Bill Dickinson a lean irregular-featured plater in his middle forties and very popular with most of the gang.

"Dickie," announced the Chargeman, "this is your new mate for a bit. Make sure you keep him at it."

For some reason, I learned, the affable, composed journeyman preferred his nickname to William or Bill, but in any event I took to him from the start.

"Hello mate!" he greeted me with a smile, holding out his hand. "We'll soon get used to one another. That's my sack truck and tools and wherever we go you follow me round with it. First thing this morning we fix up a set of hanging bars."

I felt as if a great weight had suddenly lifted from my shoulders. At long last I was about to help with something really creative, turning the crude shape of a frame with bits and pieces attached 117 and an asbestos-covered boiler resting inside, into the likeness of a locomotive. It was a *Hall* class 4900 we were to work on, and after enlisting the help of the overhead crane to temporarily attach the long central bars to their hanging brackets, went off to collect from the driller the curved end bars which gave the cab and front end their graceful shape and assemble them all with butt straps ready for the hydraulic riveter.

I soon realised I was lucky to be with the most accomplished plater on the gang, and I believe in his quiet way Dickie grew to appreciate me without making it too obvious. I was now a ready, anxious learner and once having gained confidence could be trusted to get on with a job when left with it. After the first couple of weeks this proved quite often, for Bill Dickinson had one or two habits from which nobody was going to change him.

Of all things, he was another one who relished a long gossip and once he'd got the current job under way, would wander off and leave me for anything up to half an hour. I always wanted to know where he could be located should anything go wrong, and would usually see him standing in a small group perhaps passing a smutty joke or two (of these he was quite fond!) and passing round a small battered snuff box, his other peculiarity. Whenever there was a lull he would pull this out, tap the lid a couple of times, open it up and sniff one or two whiffs up each nostril. He offered me a pinch early on and not wishing to be rude I indulged; but only once, for it brought on a sneezing attack which caused the journeyman great amusement! Of course he always returned quickly to the job when word got around the Foreman was about. But our Chargeman never bothered him.

"D'you think we could get on with it Dickie?" he would ask tentatively, in the hope of breaking up the little gathering, but Dickie would reply: "Yes, just letting the sweat go back. Be there in a minute."

When he eventually returned he would ask: "Getting on all right mate? Any trouble? The answer more often was "No", and Bill Dickinson might go on: "Never let our Chargeman scare you mate. You're doing a good job and between us we more than pull our weight compared with some on this gang. 'E can't tell me anything about my job. I was doing plating more or less before 'e 'ad an 'ole in 'is arse, excuse my language. Done nothing but

118

boiler work all his life, and he knows it really. 'E's not so bad mind you, just gets a bit flappable when things don't go quite right."

He might swear more often than I liked, but it was the easy-flowing habitual defamations spoken without real malice in most workshops and, in my case, could be comfortably overlooked in view of all I was learning, not only about plating and the various ways of tackling a puzzling job, but also about life in general.

When the hanging bars were eventually riveted the cab had to be slid into place over the boiler and brought to settle on the rear, curved hanging bars. This operation was often tricky, for the cab was lowered down from the small hook of the huge overhead crane by means of rope slings then levered into place with crowbars, with me on one side and Bill Dickinson on the other, later to be secured in position with snap-head bolts and nuts, more often than not all left to me.

Following this the running plates, which had been marked off and punched in advance must be temporarily bolted either side the length of the boiler and their ⅝in. holes reamed out with a pneumatic drill. The two of us, one holding and operating the machine the other gripping the projecting arm to prevent it 'kicking', would quickly go along the length of the plates with a tapered, fluted reamer and extension to clear all the holes, pouring oil on the tool at intervals to prevent it overheating.

When all this was achieved and the plates riveted down the curved front end must be plated, and I enjoyed this most of all, since some skill was required in rolling the plates into the correct fit.

"Always roll them a bit more than necessary mate," advised my mentor, applying a template to test the curvature. "You can easily knock a bit of the shape out from the back, but it's a devil to knock it back in."

He made it all look so easy with a few nicely placed blows of the flogging hammer, then bedding the plates down so that the holes married up using the hand hammer and a couple of drifts, but when he let me have a turn I was astonished how difficult it was. Practice makes perfect, and this proved to be so. Finally the six splashers must be fixed in place with ⅜in. snapheads, spring washers and nuts. When these popular 4-6-0s were eventually wheeled and approaching completion at the bottom end of the Shop, I might go down and admire our joint handiwork, with a slight pride I once thought my apprenticeship would never bring me.

Bull-nosed King Henry VII *on a Swindon to Bristol local, March 1935*

Other occupations

14

This successful partnership also gave me opportunities to move around the AE and watch more closely the work of the fitters. It was always interesting to see one of the 4-6-0s lifted up and carefully set down on its driving wheels. First the axle-boxes, those items I was always hearing so much about at home as a boy, were assembled on their axles and the wheels spaced out in readiness. Next, lifted from the stands on which it had rested the frame with the boiler would come along swaying slightly in the clutches of the 100-ton crane, hover over the site, then come down boldly until within a fraction of the hornblocks into which the axle-boxes were to fit; then there were minor adjustments to the wheel positions. How the craneman high up in his yellow box could distinguish the signals of his groundsman (better known as the hooker-on) defeated me, for stooping over intently the latter would bend a couple of fingers which was all that was necessary for the crane driver to lower his huge charge barely perceptibly.

"Hold it!" might come the cry from one of the fitters at the axle-boxes underneath, and Tom the groundsman would give a sharp blow on the whistle held between his teeth.

"Carry on!" would yell the fitter, then with another flick of the fingers there would be another infinitesimal drop until each pair of hornblocks made contact with their axle-boxes, so that it was now a gradual easy descent until the frame had settled. The hornties must now be bolted in position, then out from underneath came the whole bunch of fitters as the crane lifted the engine clear of the pit for a rotation of the wheels until the crank pins were in line; then it was "all hands on deck" to lift the heavy shiny coupling rods and coax them into place. With the new aligning equipment this was rarely any problem, and when one side was fixed the operation on the other side of the locomotive was much easier.

Still another innovation while I worked there was the installation of a valve-setting machine. When most of the moving parts were in place the valves must be accurately set. This was normally done by inching the driving wheels along with angled pinch bars specially shaped at their ends, a labourer on each wheel levering the bar in unison with the others, rather like slaves on a Roman galley, with the valve-setter controlling the operation in the engine pit when working on internal cylinders, by means of a shrill whistle. This tedious operation was obviated when one pit was taken over and converted into a valve-setting machine designed and built in the Works which could take up to an eight-coupled engine on its adjustable rollers. Since it was electrically operated with an inching control either from the pit or from outside it, this resulted in considerable saving in time and labour.

Between the building of 4-6-0s there was the endless procession of 0-6-0 tank engines or 0-4-2 side tank locomotives, and I always watched with interest when the next pair of frames arrived and were laid flat for the marking-out to see what kind of work was in store.

In due course a pair of 5000 *Castle* frames were set down and I could hardly wait for them to be propped up in their stands with cross members and internal cylinder castings fitted, then the rear ends built up and hanging brackets added so that my mate and I could start on our own contribution.

With this class a new type of light-plate casing was required to cover the internal valves at the front, underneath the boiler, and these had to be made up and assembled by us with the help of the welder, then fitted before the immaculate locomotive left the workshop, gleaming in its masterly applied livery, brass beading, copper-capped chimney and proud number and name plates. 5033, *Broughton Castle* was the first I worked on and the second—I could hardly wait for the name to be fixed over the central driving wheel—was *Corfe Castle*!

Later a new design of two-cylinder 4-6-0 was developed during my two years with Bill Dickinson, the 6800 *Granges*. This involved reading working drawings and making jigs for the drillers; and when the hanging bars were assembled on the prototype there was the careful marking off of the running plates to be done and templates made from these. The curved front-end plates had to be marked off blank, carefully centre-punched, then rolled flat again to become further templates. It was challenging and painstaking work on which Bill Dickinson allowed me to take a good share of responsibility.

1935 was indeed an interesting time in the AE Shop for two more developments were carried out. I was always amazed at the crude way speeds were estimated on the G.W.R. by timing with stop watches between marked points alongside the lines, when even the earliest motor cars had speedometers. This omission on the railway was first rectified on a batch of *Castles* and then became standard equipment. The mechanism was activated by the right-hand trailing wheel, a dial being fixed in the cab just below the driver's lookout window and set up to avoid excessive vibration and give a steady reading. Unfortunately they were said to be rather fallible and prone to give a higher reading than was the case, causing a number of drivers to ease down and arrive late!

The other development was considerably more hush-hush and involved the two express engines, 6014 *King Henry VII* and 5005 *Manorbier Castle*. These were brought to a corner of the workshop, and though great attempts were made at secrecy, peculiar shapes began to appear alongside the pits where they stood until the mystery was no more; it became obvious some attempt was being made at streamlining. Since it was mostly plating involved I felt aggrieved that our gang had not been commissioned to carry out the work, but as it was all light plating only sheet-metal workers and trusted fitters were chosen. When the fruits of their labours were completed there was consternation and considerable amusement from all those not directly involved.

It appeared the Directors of the Railway at Paddington were pressing the C.M.E. at Swindon to embark on streamlining against his will, and the story later went the rounds that he sent an office boy into town to buy a quantity of Plasticine and moulded it with his hands around a model of a *King* class locomotive standing on his desk, filling in all the places where there might be backstream or drag, then stuck a round blob on the front of the boiler and sent it to the Drawing Office with orders to produce a design for both a *Castle* and a *King*.

Whether the story was true or not it certainly seemed plausible to the workmen as we gazed on the finished articles in the A Shop grotesquely adorned almost beyond recognition with bits and pieces behind the chimney stack and safety valve, around the   123 cylinders and front of the cab. It looked to us all exactly what it was—a bodged-up job—and this was borne out when the novelty had exhausted itself and first the cylinder shrouds disappeared because of lack of access and overheating, and the remaining other pieces were whittled away until only the pot-bellies jutted out at the front of the boilers.

When the first Gresley streamlined Pacific *Silver Link* appeared on the L.N.E.R. later the same year, some of the more knowledgeable fitters told me Mr. C. B. Collett let slip a glorious opportunity to keep the G.W.R. in the forefront by not producing a purpose-built streamlined *Castle* or *King* in place of the two demeaning efforts that took shape instead.

Although the Factory was still not working Saturday mornings with some departments still very short of work, one profitable source of activity for our gang was the conversion of a number of 2-8-0 side tank 4200s and 5200s into a 2-8-2 wheel arrangement with an extended rear frame and enlarged bunker holding two extra tons of coal and renumbered 72XX, so giving the class a comparable range to that of a tender engine.

I never enjoyed the initial operation of cutting down the rear end with a heavy pneumatic 'cannon' of the type used in the Boiler Bay. Often I had the more dangerous part, holding the set on the rivets as the gun pounded away, hands protected with coarse gloves and eyes with goggles, but occasionally my journeyman would let me take over control of the trigger, which was still quite arduous because of the exertion essential to prevent a 'backfire' of the gun. The assembly of the new bunker and cab top presented no difficulty except the bolting down of the former to the frame with ¾in. water-tight bolts, using tar-string grummets and an unusually long extension claw-spanner.

Although far from being enamoured with my apprenticeship, working so harmoniously with such a competent easy-going character encouraged me to take more interest in the work of the Factory generally. Sometimes I must journey to the Q Shop where the blacksmith involved was required to modify a curved hanging bar, front or rear end, that wouldn't quite fit. I always enjoyed the stay and admired the cool manner of these men as they went about their work; the extraction of glowing pieces of metal from the lively furnaces, the fusing or shaping of parts with a display of shooting sparks achieved with regulated blows from the smith's mate—the striker—on the particular tool controlled by his superior, who invariably finished things off with his smaller hammer and customary ringing flourishes on the anvil.

On one occasion I stepped inside the clean orderly Pattern Shop, where the most skilled of all wood-workers were at their benches working out or painstakingly assembling the numerous intricate shapes depicted in reduced scale on the drawings in front of them. Not only must these patterns be of identical shape, but must be made to a specific and accurate oversize to allow for the shrinkage of the molten metal as it cools. I had the feeling of being gazed upon with some suspicion, and knowing no one with whom I could pretend to have business I took my leave soon after as if I had made some mistake.

In contrast to this was the J Shop, or Iron Foundry, where I could always find an excuse to visit Ron Parker's father. This workshop with its extensive stone façade running parallel to the main railway line must surely be one of the quietest engineering ones in the whole Factory, with its dirt floor and scanty machinery. It was fascinating to see the men working over their moulds in shirt sleeves with such patience and care, patting and fussing at the sand to make sure it conformed tightly to the wooden pattern, then when eventually satisfied, easing the latter out with the utmost caution. If the sand were in the least disturbed they would smooth it back gently into place with something resembling a little home-made brush dipped in what looked like water.

When all was ready, down at the far end of the Foundry the belly of one of the roaring cupolas would be tapped for a stream of dangerous liquid metal to spew forth into the waiting ladle. I was even lucky enough to see the casting of an internal cylinder block for a *Castle* nearing completion, its hollow form sunk into the soft floor and the molten metal being carefully poured in by two men controlling the ugly heavy ladle by means of hand wheels, as it hung from the overhead crane, a third man all the while carefully smoothing back with a long skimmer from the lip of the cauldron the darker slag that floated on the surface. The casting would then be left for a few days to thoroughly cool out. Further along, on the Shop floor, was a similar finished casting 125 in the process of being cleaned up by the fettlers, and as I studied its intricate design more closely I realised what skill was involved on the part of both pattern-maker and moulder to bring such a large and vital component to reality. The Foundry was a place of grimy, sweating men, its artisans smooth and quietly efficient. Impressive though it all was, every time I came away I considered myself fortunate not to be one of their calling.

Periodically I also made visits to the Central Boiler Station that supplied the whole Loco Works with steam, its eight splendid water-tube boilers with their slow-moving, automatic, chain-grate stokers and pulverised fuel a genuine source of interest since they were a subject of my studies at Night School. Their chimneys were a landmark for miles around, made up as they were of discarded boiler barrels of the 2300 class locos bolted end to end to a height of 80 feet; while alongside one of them and atop their steam pipes were the large twin cups of the famous hooter, regulating Swindon time at set periods of the working day, drawing employees to their labours from all parts of the town and beyond. When the Foremen left at knocking-off time the workmen always congregated near the Shop exit, and those in sight of the hooter would watch intently for the first tell-tale wisps of steam warming the cups immediately prior to the blast, hoping to be first off the mark, ahead of the flood-like surge that would immediately follow. Indeed there almost seemed some rivalry in this connection.

While there it was difficult to resist wandering into the adjoining Rolling Mills to watch the long white snakes of gleaming metal sizzling through the rolls, sliding back and forth through the graded corrugations until the required shape was accomplished, then to be slung with tongs onto the already dying pile at one side of the machine.

Beyond the Mills again was the Steam Hammer Shop. Here I might wait patiently until one of the furnaces yawned open, its door balanced on heavy counterweights, to reveal the near-blinding inferno that raged within and from which would be extracted, by means of special tongs supported by chains hanging from a swivel frame, a dazzling white-hot billet. This was swung round to the anvil, the mouth of the furnace closing behind it, and under the direction of the smith the hammer-man would begin his

126

Sawing hot iron in F Shop

precise leverage of the handle controlling the massive hammerhead. Down it would plunge with a spurt of steam, shuddering the ground again and again as it remorselessly pounded the tortured ingot into a more elongated shape, throwing cascades of sputtering sparks in all directions, just a momentary pause now and then to allow the accumulating dark scale to be brushed aside with a large kind of besom.

When the smith was satisfied with this initial stage, in would go the crude dull-red mass for a further intense reheating, then out again in due course to be subjected to a finer, less violent forging and turning until it took on the rough but recognisable contours of a coupling or connecting rod, or some other item of heavy machinery. As a spectacle for visitors sometimes a pocket watch might be placed on the anvil block and the huge hammer-weight would plummet down with a hiss and a snort to halt within a cardboard thickness of the glass, such was the skill of the operator.

On these excursions in slack times, I inevitably carried a pencil on me and a piece of paper held noticeably in my hand, so that should anyone that mattered be approaching I could stop and pretend to be making a few notes. Indeed, it was a well-established fact that with a sheet of white paper held prominently and a purposeful walk, the freedom of the whole Works was yours from one end to the other, including the Carriage and Wagon side, without a single challenge—all 320 acres!

First aid

15

My earliest acquaintance with first aid happened as a young lad when I obtained, possibly by schoolboy barter, a square pocket-sized, somewhat battered, black manual with a faded St. John emblem on its front. Inside the cover was a sketch of a skeleton with the medical names of the major bones of the body which I quickly learned off. Interspersed with its text were numerous diagrams of the various methods of bandaging used for the injured, and the more I studied them the keener I became.

I eventually resolved that should I ever be 'lucky' enough to encounter an accident I must be capable of dealing with it, and to that end got hold of a suitable tin and started to build up my own first aid kit. One of my last necessities was a one-inch roller bandage, but these cost 1d which I could ill afford, and when I mentioned this to my father he pacified me by saying: "I'll see if I can get one off the ambulance fella inside."

I was not certain he meant it because I had to nag him for well over a week, his excuse being he "hadn't managed to catch him yet". Dad was on night shift at the time and I was despairing so much of acquiring this vital item, I had given up asking him each time he came home; then one morning as I was about to clean my shoes before trotting off to school I put my hand in the toe of one and found a lump stuck in there. Sure enough, it was a one-inch bandage in a grubby packet, and now that my kit was complete, at least in my esteem, I could have kissed my father.

Some weeks later I was in church one Sunday morning when a young lady in front of me was carried out in a fainting condition. I could see them trying to revive her in the church porch and lost all further interest in the service trying to remember what should be done according to my little Black Book. To my absolute disgust the memory failed and the mind went blank! I was so angry, I went home afterwards, took my book up to my back bedroom and did my best to learn off by heart the treatment of a faint (correct name syncope!) so that I wouldn't be caught out again.

The author in a first aid competition simulating a level-crossing accident

I knew there was a very strong first aid movement in the Factory, well-supported by the Managers and other officials, which was essential because of the numerous and occasionally fatal accidents that occurred there as in all industrial establishments on a similar scale. I remember my father coming home and telling my mother that one poor fellow had been caught up in a huge planing machine and killed instantly; while another dreadful accident happened in his own machine shop when an unfortunate man sitting astride his grinding machine was near decapitated when the grindstone burst.

"Everybody stopped work in the Shop," my father said, "and after a while a lot of us went up to have a look, but by golly I wish I hadn't. The poor fellow's brains were splashed over the wall, and nobody knew what to do. Then Bill Towner went up with a triangular bandage and wrapped it over the remains of his head, then some more ambulance men came along and took him away. I tell you, when we set out of a morning you never know what's going to happen by night-fall."

Such sentiments worried me for a while, and when I began as an office boy I was eager to get involved in the movement, though you must be at least 16 to take the course. My father again had a word with an ambulance man he sometimes walked home with and Joe said: "Let him come to the lectures and I'll see what I can do." So each Sunday morning for eight weeks I went to the Staff Association Hall in Bridge Street where one of the doctors from the Medical Fund more or less read the Black Book to a hundred of us and perhaps more.

I enjoyed it immensely until the time came for the examination which was held in the Mess Room in London Street, the long, low, dingy quarters of numerous cycle racks and endless round stanchions supporting the workshops above; here we carried out the practical work under instructors two evenings a week. While one section of this drab part of the Factory was still used for 'messing', the other half had been sealed off and outside working hours was allowed to be used by Great Western first aid employees as a practice room.

The doctor taking the examination was a very mild-mannered man (some of them I learnt could be blunt, impatient and almost frightening) from Wootton Bassett, and I thought I answered the

130

theory questions reasonably well since one of them was on fainting, of all things!

"Now I want to you do up the patient for a dressing on the head and a fractured patella," he said. I coped with the first quite comfortably, but when I considered the fracture my mind went completely blank once again. Fortunately Joe, my sponsor, had volunteered as my patient and was as keen for me to get through as I was to pass. Sensing my dilemma he fixed his eyes on the examiner sat at the table with the next candidate and whispered through his teeth: "Get that bloody splint and put it at the back of my leg . . . now put the padding under my heel and lift . . ."

Joe left off with his eyes still on the doctor and I gathered why. I proceeded to do as he said. "Now fold a narrow bandage," hissed Joe when the time was opportune, "and tie it round my thigh . . . Now another round the leg." It was beginning to come back at last. There was a figure of eight to be put round the knee and a tricky bandage to secure the foot and splint which Joe couldn't help me with because the doctor was now approaching. I knew it wasn't correct and I had a numbing feeling I was going to fail. "H'm not too bad," observed the doctor to my surprise. "It wouldn't do any harm, if not too much good."

I walked home with Joe feeling I'd rather let him down. "That was a near one," he remarked. "What went wrong?"

"I don't know," I replied. "Somehow I just couldn't think. I remember exactly what to do now."

"Too damn late," retorted Joe. "But you answered the questions pretty well. You'll get through. But don't let on to anybody you're under age or I'll be in real trouble."

Joe's confidence proved justified and when I went up to get my very first certificate at the elaborate prize-giving complete with concert at the Baths Hall in front of the Managers and officials seated on the platform, it was one of the most embarrassing yet at the same time proudest moments of my life so far.

Thus began an interest I was determined to pursue throughout my apprenticeship. You were not allowed access to the tall red first aid boxes around the workshops until you took a second exam the following year, and I could hardly wait until the precious common key was placed in my hand and, although only a mere youth, I gained the title of 'First Aid Man'.

My services in the AE Shop were rarely called upon in the earlier days except by fellow apprentices because there were so many experienced fellow members about, but not all of these took an examination regularly nor were as efficient as they should be. I well remembered one accident where a labourer slipped on a grating and was caught by the capstan on the rapidly moving traversing table and had a huge lump of flesh gouged from his calf. To my astonishment a leading fitter, a so-called 'qualified' man who never appeared at a practice, took out a large piece of lint from the portable cabinet and soaked it in iodine before smacking it on the ugly wound. I wanted to shout that it must never be done and was amazed that more capable men stood by and watched. But there was an unwritten rule that whoever was first on the case was allowed to carry on unless help was solicited. Apart from the extra shock to the injured victim, iodine, I was always told, must be allowed to dry before it is covered, as it could possibly cause a nasty burn.

I soon became persuaded to enter into competition work and joined a Beginners' Team, which consisted of members who had never won a contest except for the Captain of the group. We were given numbers: 1 being the Captain, 2 always going to the head of the patient, 4 to the feet while No. 3 assisted the Captain at the middle on the opposite side. After a few preliminary tests I was given the responsibility of No. 3 amounting almost to Deputy Captain, and was determined to prove worthy of it.

Because I didn't want anyone to see me reading direct from the manual and think I lacked confidence I wrote out word for word on separate sheets of folded paper every chapter in the Book, carried one of these into the works with me each day and in that five to eight minutes before things began sat alone on the sack truck of our tools with my feet resting on the handles and read and read until I could quote it all verbatim. When I compared it with the Black Book back at home it all came back so easily I could even quote all page numbers as well.

In the competitions there was always a team test where we were engaged jointly in restoring a patient under the critical eye of a doctor examiner, and then individual tests usually for each pair. Fortunately the Captain was with No. 2 for the latter while I was paired with No. 4. Dare I say we won the competition on our first entry and were no longer classed as 'Beginners'! But watching our test was one of the keenest competition men in the whole Works whose dedicated ambition was to win the supreme award of the G.W.R. at Paddington, as the winners of the Directors' Shield. He was looking for two more conscientious members and invited my Captain and myself to link up with him. It was regular practice at the Mess Rooms three times a week including Sunday mornings and further swotting on the Black Book to ensure word perfection. No. 5 was the patient and the reserve who didn't participate in the actual competition but was entitled to a prize if his team gained one. How the long-suffering fellow was mauled about! Yet he never complained, not even if he finished up unrecognisable and more like an Egyptian mummy.

Given a card reading something like this: "You four are approaching a house where a man is painting a window on a short ladder. He gives a shout and falls to the ground. Act as you should. Time allowed 15 minutes." Then the conversation would ebb and flow along these lines:

"Any further danger?" "No."

"I speak to the patient. Does he answer?" "No."

"Is he breathing?" "Yes."

"Is there any bleeding?" "Yes."

"Where?" "From the right leg."

"Is it profuse?" "No."

"I examine the leg. Is there an irregularity, swelling or deformity?" And so on, with the kind person running us through with a marking sheet in his hand. All very artificial and stilted, of course, but it gave one a standard method of approach which could come naturally when faced with a real accident with casualties.

This was my real hope in pursuing the subject so assiduously, even to the occasional detriment of my evening classes at the College. As I have already mentioned, following my mother's death, I felt so keenly I wanted to be more useful in the world and of benefit to others, and in this way I was sublimating my hopeless desire of being a doctor or something like it.

Our new team quickly won a reputation in Swindon. The G.W.R. system was divided into Ambulance Districts each of which held its own First Aid Competition, the winners of which 133 competed in a rather privately held semi-final. Our semi-final was always held in Bristol and there was speculation as we travelled back in the train, having been given an extra free pass and day off with pay, as to how we had fared, since the results were never made known until more than a week later.

We were filled with pride and perhaps over-confidence when we qualified for the final at Paddington at our first attempt, but alas we only came within the first four.

"Never mind," our Captain consoled us as we headed back to Swindon. "We made a good impression for a first time. We're knocking at the door, and we'll keep knocking till we get there." He was a placid well-respected first aider in whom we all had the greatest confidence and though we were not to attain the coveted major trophy we took part in the final each time until we were runners-up.

By this time I had gained some acceptance in the AE Shop as a "fairly good" ambulance man and found myself sought out sometimes even by the odd fitter for an ability to bandage a finger-top without it coming off too soon! Only once so far had I taken a patient out to the Medical Fund Hospital on the peculiar litter for such emergencies with its large, frail, bicycle-type wheels, namely a fellow apprentice who had broken his foot. Most men detested being pushed out on such primitive contrivances, chiefly because it always attracted attention and made them feel so ridiculous when almost everybody stopped to watch as the casualty passed up through the workshop; whenever this crude mode of transport was inevitable they much preferred to sit up on the thing if at all possible; as my patient did until we were well clear of prying eyes.

My hopes of responding satisfactorily to a call from suffering humanity were partially fulfilled one wet October election night. Dad was returning from his customary visit to the Reading Rooms of the local branch of the Mechanics Institute when he heard a terrific crash on the cross-roads at the next street to ours. He took one look and dashed home, arriving quite breathless.

"Quick Hugh! . . . Come at once . . . There's been a crash . . . outside Clark's shop!"

I had the presence of mind to grab my, now more elaborate, first aid box and ran up to the corner in the pouring rain.

A car was lying on its side with a woman passenger still within, groaning and semi-conscious, her face cut in several places. Several people were standing around speculating what should be done, among them a neighbour opposite us, a Labour canvasser who knew me and my interest well. He pushed the others aside and let me get to her.

I tried to reassure her but she was too dazed and shocked to understand much. I tied her legs together and instructed two of the others how to assist in carrying her into the nearby shop which had accommodatingly opened its door. I bathed her face and dressed it, further immobilised her legs one of which I was sure was injured, dressed a damaged hand and put it in a sling. I rode in the ambulance with the driver of the car who was also badly shaken and left my address should it be needed.

I was a little taken aback when a report of the incident appeared in the *Evening Advertiser* the following night and our neighbour was attributed with all the credit for "rendering valuable assistance", with no mention of my attempt to succour the patient. Yet inwardly I felt I had played a useful part in my first serious accident, though I subsequently learned the patient had sustained a simple fracture of the ribs which I'd failed to diagnose. Several weeks later a certain lady called at home while I was out, saying she'd come across my name while recovering in hospital, and though remembering nothing of the accident she wanted to thank me for what I had done.

It made me more aware than ever that those many hours of study and regular practice were not in vain, and though a life may not have been at risk in that instance, I must continue to keep myself well-versed and qualified so that should such a rare call present itself I would never be found wanting.

This could well have happened one cold and miserable foggy morning in January 1936. I arrived in the workshop to learn that an express train had crashed at Shrivenham some five miles to the east and there could be a large number of casualties. I also discovered two of my older and more experienced ambulance colleagues had already been called to the scene and wondered how many more of us might be needed; but no further requests were forthcoming. Much as I longed to be there, what I didn't appreciate at the time of course was that both these first aiders 135 were also skilled fitters and had become involved because they were also on an emergency breakdown gang roster.

All that day the news of the calamity hung over the A Shop like a pall and was the prevailing topic of conversation. Rumour followed rumour. The driver was killed outright and many others; then the driver and some others with a number injured; then the driver and two others, with a few injured including the fireman. I felt too restless and frustrated to get on with my work as I should, and before setting off for Night School that evening, stocked up my large cycle headlamp with fresh carbide and water to ensure it would last, and warned my father I might well be home much later than usual, but not to worry. When the evening session at the College was over I dashed out to the cycle rack promptly, wrapped myself up warmly and set off into the chill murky night, making for the long Shrivenham Road but having no idea where I would eventually finish up. My carbide-gas lamp threw a bright, wide but not very penetrating beam as I kept near the railway as best I could, passing eventually alongside its high embankment until the road passed obliquely under it. I soon had to turn down a by-road on the right and must have gone along for another mile or so before I finally came to the scene.

Laying on her side across both sets of rails like some crippled monster the maimed locomotive was a sorry sight, its front end flattened, mangled and twisted beyond recognition, while thrown to one side were the remains of a goods guard's van and several pairs of jumbled wagon wheels. Voices occasionally drifted along on the still air and shadowy outlines appeared and disappeared in the glare of the lights from time to time. A few other onlookers were likewise mutely surveying the awesome scene, as I was.

Apparently that morning, we all learned later, the coupling had snapped on a goods train out of Swindon and four coal-laden wagons and the guard's van had gradually slid to a standstill, while the rest of the train trundled on heedlessly; even the signalman in the Shrivenham box failing to notice in the fog the absence of the tell-tale red lamp indicating the train was complete—the only time in railway procedure that such a lamp indicates all is well. Meanwhile the guard applied his hand brake, assuming his train had pulled up in the loop to allow the Penzance to Paddington Sleeping Car Train, due to leave Swindon at 5.27

a.m., to have its clear run; then he peered out into the fog and realised he was still on the main line.

Knowing the Penzance Sleeper was due any moment he grabbed his detonators, it was said, and ran back at the side of the line to give warning of impending disaster. It was too late. For the express, drawn by 6007 *King William III*, was gathering speed as the driver notched up the reversing handle, having already passed the distant Shrivenham signal with his ATC bell ringing the all-clear in the cab reassuringly, only to rush past the guard and crash almost instantly into the solid obstruction of the braked van and its four heavily-laden wagons. The devastating impact snapped the coupling between the second and third trucks, shooting the leading two along the line for nearly a mile and alerting the signalman as they sped by that something was seriously wrong. He promptly put all his boards at danger, but the damage had been done; for 6007 had already reared up, mounted the guard's van and plummeted over onto the permanent way in a mass of splintered debris, tortured steel and hissing steam, dragging its tender and the two leading coaches with it.

Miraculously, only the unfortunate driver was killed instantly, impaled by the reversing lever as he was working the cut-off, and one passenger, ten others being injured in varying degrees. All the casualties were dealt with expeditiously by the time daylight broke upon the scene; while the following day 6007 was in the AE Shop extension being gravely studied by some of the men who'd helped to turn her out in her splendid livery for the very first time some nine years previously.

I took in that sombre sight for a while longer, then cycling home now with ears stinging and eyes smarting from the cold, I somehow felt justified in going out to witness firsthand the result of a rare fatal railway accident on the Great Western system, accepted as the safest in the country. But my thoughts turned also, and for many days afterwards, to that hapless engineman no doubt so proud of his handsome locomotive, edging her up to nearly 50 m.p.h., unaware it was hurtling him and the other innocent victims to imminent destruction or injury; and through no dereliction of duty on his part.

Fate takes most unpredictable and exceptionally cruel twists at times, I concluded.

Visitors to the Works and Black Friday

16

As I predicted, with three incomes and careful budgeting our family was slowly growing clear of debt and we could see the time approaching when all our necessities need no longer be obtained by instalments but saved up for and paid by cash. Our father's Balance was still lamentably poor—somehow his Chargeman simply couldn't cope—but my contribution and that of my younger sister, who seemed reasonably satisfied with her employment in the clothing factory at Shepherd Street, helped to make up the deficiency.

Therefore the year after my mother died the rest of us decided our young housekeeper deserved a good break for the splendid way she was keeping the home firmly together at considerable sacrifice to herself, and decided on a Trip Holiday Week at Paignton, once again. Our previous landlady there was fully booked so we obtained a random address from *Holiday Haunts* and were lucky in securing apartments at our first attempt. There were all the customary preliminaries to the holiday, the early rising on Trip Friday and the walk with the cases to the Dean Street entrance to obtain seats on the special train lined up for the crowds of workers and their families.

However, on arriving at our lodgings we suffered something of a shock when the landlady opened the door, for she had all the appearance of being well into her 80s!

"Come in m'dears!" she greeted us briskly. "Make yourselves at home." Then perhaps sensing our reaction she added: "Take no notice o' me. I might be 91, but I'm still alive and kicking, thank the Lord!"

We were shown into a large front room, at least it might have appeared so had it not been crowded with so much paraphernalia. As the days went on, for want of something to do during meals my sisters and I amused ourselves by counting the blue china plates adorning the walls, and variously arrived at numbers between 82 and 85! The aspidistras were easier to account for, eight large 139 thriving plants; and the number of tables amounted to six. Although every effort was taken to make us comfortable we were slightly uneasy throughout the week with the feeling we were an imposition on the dear old lady and her husband, two years older than herself.

This did not prevent us from becoming most friendly and one day our landlord invited us to see the garden "with a Channel view". We were completely staggered to find over 90 quite steep, wide stone steps looming ahead of us, so forbidding in fact father decided to withdraw from the ascent. Strenuous though it was the vista of the sparkling sea with seemingly toy steamers in the far distance was worth the effort. When we eventually got down we were greeted with: "Nice, isn't it? Can't get up there now as often as I'd like. But manage to take the washing up of a Monday, with Dad's help. Such good drying. Gives them a good airing."

Most of the week we spent leisurely on Goodrington Sands, and on our return all agreed it had been a memorable and enjoyable occasion in more ways than one, and well worth while.

This improvement in our financial position also relieved dad and myself of a regular chore—collecting the firewood from the Factory. For this tickets were issued in the shop offices and charges deducted from the wages, one fortnight a hundredweight of refuse being available and the following one perhaps a similar amount of old timber. One neighbour a few houses along had a strong trolley on stout cast-iron wheels, and as a boy, dad and I would borrow it and set out together "to get the wood". The refuse was made up of all manner of off-cuts of new wood including a fair amount of bark and was collected from Bristol Street under the shadow of the lofty water tank, another prominent landmark. When the Factory was on four days a week there was always a winding queue of trolleys and push carts waiting sometimes more than an hour for the allocation of wood.

The old timber was a far better proposition, since it was well seasoned wood from scrapped wagons and trucks and even parts of railway sleepers, and was always in great demand because it burnt so readily. For that reason it could not be obtained as often as many employees wished, and had to be collected from a square enclosure behind the high wall at the Whitehouse Bridges. Because the elevation of the road was much lower than the main railway line and the Carriage and Wagon Works running parallel, a long metal shute led down to a low wooden platform in the small yard, and as your turn at last came a large cocoa tin would be tossed down on a long string into which you placed your ticket, which was then hauled up before your ration of wood came thundering down and must be loaded on the trolley quickly before the next consignment descended. It was a regular sight in those days to see home-made trolleys and push carts of every description being trundled along the streets, a piece of timber sticking up in each corner of a trolley and the rest of the wood piled on between.

This chore, for indeed it was, in particular pushing the load up the long slope of the hazardous Rodbourne Bridges, had now become a thing of the past since it was increasingly common to hand the tickets to light hauliers who, for a modest sum, collected the wood in lots, separated by sacking, and thrust your quota over the back garden wall, the only disadvantage being that any likely-looking useful pieces of timber might never come your way; and there was no come-back since nothing could be proved!

Coal for the G.W.R. employees was ordered and paid for in the same way and delivered by the Company from two wharves, one near the Junction Station by horse and cart, and the other at the end of Rodbourne Lane from where it was more often delivered by a heavy steam wagon, which often my school pals and I would follow around fascinated by its boiler, swinging governors and large red fly-wheel. These items of wood and coal were commendable concessions, though more often than not there were complaints about the latter being: "A load of old rubbish", or: "Wot they can't damn well burn on the engines. 'Alf on it dust!"

Back in the Works, Wednesday afternoon was visiting time and without previous arrangement visitors could congregate outside the Tunnel Entrance opposite the Mechanics Institute and be taken on tour by one of the Watchmen—a chance to identify that otherwise faceless breed of people. For special large parties individual arrangements were made. Firstly in preparation, all the main thoroughfares—those labelled "Fire Engine Route, Keep Clear"—were checked and the main passage-way through each workshop on the tour cleaned up and marked with arrows. 141

Premium apprentices of wealthier forebears and ordinary fitter apprentices nearing the end of their time conducted the party around in smaller groups, stopping here and there to give an explanation. I envied them this, for it meant an early pass-out on the day, coming back in clean clothes and often being listened to attentively.

Even more interesting were the times when distinguished visitors came to Swindon with its unique reputation. Though only six and a half years old at the time I could recall lining up in Faringdon Road with crowds of other children to wave at King George V and Queen Mary as they went by in an open carriage during their visit to the town and Railway Works. Great publicity was given to their Majesties watching a welcome message being cast in the Iron Foundry and especially when, at the conclusion of the visit, they climbed aboard No. 4082 *Windsor Castle* and the King drove the impressive locomotive from outside the A Shop up to the Junction Station.

I could also recall my father extolling the visit of King Amanullah of Afghanistan in 1928 who returned to his country only to be deposed. For such visits everything of interest was laid on—a locomotive with its wheels travelling at full speed on the Testing Plant, a near-completed engine suspended from one of the four overhead cranes running up and down the long workshop, and another fully completed one at the exit for the visitor to mount and study the cab dials.

But the visit I remembered so vividly firsthand was that of Prince Alake of Abeokuta, said to be the leading Chief in Nigeria. All the usual elaborate preparations were carried out for this occasion, and it was said around the shop that Alake had to travel 30 miles down river before he arrived at civilisation, so his coming was eagerly awaited by the men in the A Shop who were instructed to keep to their work to impress him.

Presently the message spread that he had arrived at the AV Shop and I ensured I was deliberately not far away as the Prince and his entourage stopped to view the long Standard No. 12 boiler casing suspended from the high 'attic' crane, firehole uppermost, and being lowered by remote control over the monolith that rose up from the floor, being part of the heavy hydraulic machine used for riveting the barrels. They watched the process once then were escorted to the AE Shop. Standing close to his regal master who was bedecked in resplendent white and gold robes was a mighty Nubian coal-black bodyguard holding an expansive highly-decorated umbrella on a handle as tall as himself, and wherever the Prince stopped so did the umbrella over his head with the bodyguard firmly in charge. But on viewing the stately *Castle* class engine high in the air and no far away, the whites of his eyes enlarged to their utmost and there was the great umbrella clearly shaking; but his master retained his complete dignity with a cool smile.

Though the men dutifully stayed at their work places all eyes were on the exotic spectacle as the ostentatious visitors and the austere officials walked sedately down the workshop, then after mounting the footplate of an immaculate 4-6-0 via a wooden staircase, with his frustrated henchman still trying to shield his Chief with the exasperating umbrella in spite of all the obstructions, Prince Alake turned to look back from the driver's position. Immediately all the workmen including myself surged forward with cheers which the dignified ruler acknowledged, then waved for silence.

"I am very impressed with all I have seen," he said to our astonishment, in good English. "And I thank you for your kindness." There were further cheers as he climbed down the other side and was escorted through the wide doors of the workshop.

Such scintillating occasions were all too rare and some months later the dreaded rumours began to circulate. Railway "takings" were below expectations again and a "number" would have to go. Swindon being so much a one industry town, except for a few small factories employing mostly female labour, this was almost a death knell to those who feared they were vulnerable. Rumour followed rumour—500 to go from the loco side, 250 from the carriage side, then 800 and 300, then 1,000 from the loco side alone.

I had grown up with this constantly recurring threat to our meagre livelihood and the insufferable relief in our home when we knew my father had escaped yet again. In earlier days absolute power over sackings was in the hands of the Foremen who were often guilty of partiality and favouritism, but the Unions had 143 since grown stronger, formed a united front, the Syndicate, and insisted that the rule must be: "Last in, first out". Yet of course so much depended on how far back in service the dismissals would go; three years, five years, eight years? No one could be sure. Benefactor to the town the G.W.R. certainly was, but here was the penalty for such a sheer monopoloy of employment—some years on the dole until things looked up, or working away from the town and trying to keep two homes going, few manual workers possibly affording the uprooting of the family. Even the dole, in its paucity was subject to the rigorous Means Test, and barely covered food and rent, let alone other commitments.

The week of Black Friday a deepening gloom settled throughout the Works.

"How far are they going back?" they would ask.

"D'you think you'll be safe?" one would enquire of another.

"I'll tell you what, if I've got to go again, it will be the last time. I'll never come back to this place."

But of course they did; to the annoyance of the old stagers.

"Should bloody-well teach the bosses a lesson," they'd say. "If they all refused to come back it wouldn't 'appen so often. Only got t' snap their fingers and they come running. Never learn, they won't—never!"

For in spite of all its shortcomings the Factory wasn't a sweat shop unlike the two factories at Oxford; some even went as far as Luton and found the difference there as well. Such places offered higher wages, but every penny was hard earned.

So came the Friday everybody hated, for even the longer service manual workers (clerical staff were never involved in these dismissals) who considered themselves almost immune were distressed to witness what as about to happen. Around 11 o'clock the Chief Clerk would leave the Shop office with his sheet of paper and work almost immediately came to a standstill. Conscious of all eyes upon him he might make his way to the nearest man on his list and briefly say: "The Foreman would like to see you in his office."

Then the trek would commence, one after the other slowly mounting the long flight of wooden steps, waiting outside for his mutually unfortunate predecessor to emerge before doffing his 144 cap and following in to get his notice: "The Company regrets your services are no longer required after August 31st". And so soon after Trip!

"Is he coming this way?" one suspecting man would ask of his mate, not bearing to look where the Chief Clerk was going.

"Thank 'eavens 'e's gone by . . . Phew! . . . Oh my God! 'E's seen me. 'E's comin' back 'ere! Oh no!"

Oh yes! Some Foremen handled the situation as delicately as they could with a few words of sympathy and perhaps even a promise of genuine consideration when times looked up again, but others discharged the duty more casually and coldly.

I was in the Boiler Bay that morning when one artisan of about 40 returned with his note in his trembling fingers.

"What the 'ell can I do?" he asked no one in particular, his face white and drawn, his eyes red-rimmed. "Already got three kids and the missus expectin' another next month."

To see such fine, proud, hard-working men on the verge of tears and reduced to whining filled me with both embarrassment and indignation, something I was never to forget. From that day onwards I firmly pledged myself to work hard, study earnestly and resolutely plan for a future that was going to be stable and secure, even if it meant ignoring the bait of an immediate substantial increase in wages.

Characters who broke monotony

17

There was relief all round when the redundant army of workers had departed, not just because the fortunate ones left behind felt more secure, but also because the dreaded Friday and its aftermath, that ensuing week of unpleasantness and embarrassing commiserations, was at long last over. After a few months a belief might circulate that "within a year or so" things could be looking up and re-instatements begin. But "a year or so" seemed like an eternity when you and your family were right on the breadline and bare essentials were difficult to come by.

New work, replacements for old stock, was still trickling along, the sturdy and powerful 5700 pannier tank 0-6-0s intermingled with the occasional batch of *Granges* and, favourites of all, perhaps another ten *Castles*.

Meanwhile over in the Boiler Bay an area had been cleared in the top corner and a large boiler placed on its side and completely surrounded with screens marked "No Admittance". The Works Manager, Head Boiler Foreman and his welding counterpart came and went frequently and speculation began as to what was afoot, especially when boilermakers were seen going in and out of the enclosure in white burn-proof dungarees. Soon it was obvious something experimental was being conducted in secret and when the men appeared from time to time with dark goggles hanging from their necks and faces red and streaming with perspiration the mystery was out. A new method of repairing fireboxes by means of copper welding, instead of riveting, was under way.

It was most unpleasant and unhealthy work for the two welders who, in intense heat, worked simultaneously on the seam, melting a ¼in. diameter copper rod to fuse the two plates. It was so unbearably hot that they could only endure it for a limited time and must then be relieved by two others, with the heat being maintained continuously until the whole seam was finished. So cleverly was the operation worked out that the bevelled plates to be welded might be ³/₁₆in. apart at one end and 2in. at the other,   147

Knocking-off time—1

but as the welding got under way the contraction gradually drew the two edges into correct juxtaposition as the operation neared completion.

A great deal of preparation was essential in setting up this operation prior to welding, but whenever I passed and they were working in their veritable inferno I could appreciate the intolerable conditions; the heat which could be felt and the roar of the acetylene lamps, making the whole thing seem quite frightening. It was accepted as being unhealthy, and I was determined never to experience it! Yet it was another procedure that put Swindon ahead in that particular field and one more showpiece, for very special visitors only.

Again such things made me realise how lucky I was to be in the comparative tranquillity of the New Work Section in the AE and the freedom of movement that went with my work as opposed to people like my own father, stuck at the same machine all day and every day, and in the one environment of countless speeding belts and tireless machinery grinding away, shapers, millers, slotters, planers, lathes, all torturing metal into finer shapes with screeches, whines and clatter.

Then there were the various individuals I encountered and could converse with in the enclosed cabs of the tank engines, characters like Nel Hirst, said to be the biggest Liar in the A Shop! I'd heard all about him from my father in previous years and now met him in the flesh, with his wide dusky features, broad moustache and penetrating eyes.

"Killed three Germans in the War with one bullet," he told me coolly one day, one of his favourite stories. "Went straight through two of 'em, ricocheted off the wall and caught a third. Might of 'ad a fourth if 'e 'adn't ducked."

I took it all in and nodded seriously, not wishing to offend this eccentric fitter who seemed to really believe his own tall stories.

"Worked in this place some years ago," he would go on smoothly, "and couldn't make out where all the oil in this cannister was goin' to, being no sign of a leak anywhere. Decided to sit it out one night, and along came a couple o' rats. One perched on the edge, stuck 'is tail in the oil and swung it round for t'other to lick it. And damn me, when 'e'd 'ad enough, jumped up on the tin hisself and did the same thing for t'other 'un."

From time to time brighter moments also occurred on the new work pits particularly where a pair of fitters who always worked together were concerned. The Terrible Twins they might have been called, not because of any likeness in appearance since one was short and thin while the other was bulky and casual, but because of the mischief they caused and the pranks they played.

In the *Evening Advertiser* at that time was a 'children's corner' entitled *Nig Nogs*, and the phrase caught on. Each day a list of children's names was published under "Happy Birthday", and it was not unusual to see the name of some labourer or even an unpopular tradesman listed under the heading. Allied to this was the practice of 'Nig Nogging', engaging a workman or apprentice in conversation near the edge of an engine pit while a fellow conspirator down below painted the heels of his boots with red lead paint or whitening.

Poor old Lavatory Dan whose menial tasks included cleaning out the drains and urinals in the AE Shop got wise to this practice and when the solid serious-looking fitter started to chat him up, looked first down the pit and then made sure he stood four or five feet away. But not to be outdone the other half of the sportive team tied the paint brush to a long broom handle and when Dan's back was towards him manipulated the contrivance carefully until the unsuspecting labourer was branded on his boots yet again.

Another pathetic individual exploited by the two pranksters who often broke the dullness and monotony of workshop life with their light relief was Lennie Funnel, Little Len he was nicknamed because of his sturdy build. Though many years his junior, I could remember him from early school days, as he was notoriously backward and politely known as "a bit simple". However, he didn't shrink from hard work with a broom and shovel, but became an obvious target for the Terrible Two.

One day they approached Little Len and asked him if he could sing.

"Course I bloody can!" he snorted indignantly. "Wot for?"

"Well, we're just wondering. D'you know the Tonic Sol-fa?"

"Dunno, wot you mean?"

"Yes you do. You know, Doh, Ray, Me, Fah, Soh."

"Oh that. Course I do."   149

"Can you sing with us? Come on Lennie. Do-oh-oh! Ra-aye-aye! Me-eee!"

Len caught on fast, out of tune, but the others nodded encouragingly.

"You know Len," one said, "I reckon you got a future there. Taken a few singing lessons myself. Ever thought of taking it up? Better than sweeping shop floors."

"Well—not really," admitted the flattered Lennie. "Wouldn't mind though."

"Tell you what," suggested the other, "why don't you enter the talent competition at the Gaumont." This was the luxurious cinema standing at the top end of Regent Street which held talent competitions between performances at weekends.

"Don't mind if I do. Wot shall I sing?"

"D'you know *God Save the King*?"

"Course I bloody do!"

"Let's hear a bit of it then."

Len's rendering was disharmonious to say the least, and though he wasn't sure of many of the words, he plodded on.

"Bravo!" applauded the other two enthusiastically, as several of their mates looked on from a distance. "That really was something. We're going to get an audition for you Len, but first we want you to learn *Danny Boy*. We'll get the music for you."

This they did, and not only canvassed enough signatures for his entry but encouraged quite a number of fellow workers and apprentices to attend the night he appeared on stage and vote for him.

I considered the whole thing was rather cruel and only heard what happened the following Monday morning. Apparently Len came on stage attired in an ill-fitting 'best suit' and because of his rather impervious nature not in the least embarrassed. To say his interpretation of the ballad sounded painful was being quite generous, while his attempts to reach the higher notes obviously caused him some distresss. However, his supporters around the auditorium clapped and cheered so much that the rest of the audience saw the joke and joined in enthusiastically, and to the Manager's consternation he had no alternative but to award Lennie first prize for the evening.

150   There was no holding the aspiring Caruso throughout the

ensuing week, for whenever the opportunity arose with no Foremen about Lennie was asked to render *Danny Boy* to all and sundry and did so with great gusto to the detriment of what few vocal chords he possessed, but to warm applause and suppressed laughter. In due course it dawned on the "Canary", as he was also nicknamed, that he'd been taken for a very long ride, and he turned quite nasty and most aggressive towards the instigators of his fiasco and anyone else who ventured to taunt him.

One other character worthy of mention was the Chargehand Labourer, Sandy Hopkins, in the Boiler Bay. His was a slightly drooping figure because of one short leg, and this affliction together with his fair untidy moustache didn't contribute much to a commanding presence as regards those under him; but he tried his gentle best. Even the Foreman might take advantage of the easily-harassed and constantly apprehensive Sandy, administering a false ticking off or sending him on some fruitless errand, then chuckling after him as he trundled away.

Further, it was said the little Chargehand had a slight domestic problem. Being worth more than his station in society and general appearance suggested, he'd married later in life, his partner being a much younger woman to whom, apparently, at some time in their courtship he must have confided exactly what he was worth. By all accounts she was a flashy but very restless blonde who, without consulting her trusting spouse, would do a 'moonlight flit' during the day, moving house to another part of the town, so that when Sandy arrived 'home' a note would be pinned to the door informing him: "Moved to 40 Barton Street" or some such-like address and the hapless man would have to trudge off to find it. By all accounts this happened not infrequently; but perhaps what was not quite as true was the tale going the rounds of the AV that the chickens Sandy kept in his back garden got so used to being shunted around place to place, they only had to hear the pantechnicon draw up at the front door and they would lay passively on their backs, put their feet together, then wait patiently for their legs to be tied!

Whether this account ever got back to the harmless Chargehand I never knew, but though frequently at someone else's expense, such stories considerably helped the day along.

152

Knocking-off time—2

The Boiler Bay and dismissal

18

Each year now as Trip came round our family was able to indulge in the luxury of a week's holiday away from home, though our individual choice might differ. One year I visited Cornwall with my trusted friend Ron Parker, using Truro as a centre and exploring all that lovely corner of the extreme South West. The following year when Ron cried off rather too late to cancel the arrangements I took Jane to Ilfracombe and toured all that attractive area of North Devon.

A few months later, soon after my twentieth birthday, further changes took place in the Boiler department of the Works. The Senior Foreman, my distant relation, retired, and our Foreman being next in line in seniority succeeded to the post, taking with him his close Chargeman with a promotion to Junior Foreman.

The new man sent down to take over the AV came from the L2 Shop which specialised in locomotive tenders and outstation tank and civil construction work, while to replace the departed Chargehand, Sid Matthews had been already installed in the tall 'black box'. Within a week or so he came round to see me.

"I want you to understand I've got nothing to do with this," he began, "but the new Foreman says all apprentices got to be moved round more, and that you've been here too long. He wants you to report to the Boiler Bay next Monday. I tried to keep you, but there it is. Sorry."

Since I am forced to admit I could never really bring myself to trust the new Chargeman I didn't somehow feel he was sorry to see me go, for at 20 my wage was now quite fair and something a younger apprentice wouldn't command. Yet I appreciated the point that boilermaker apprentices should be moved around and monitored just as their fitter counterparts were; furthermore, I'd done extremely well to escape the Bay for so long, attributing this partly to my consistent attendance at night school, which I had now dropped after obtaining the City and Guilds Certificate for my trade.

153

I wasn't in the least interested in boiler work of any kind, but was relieved to find I was detailed not to the cutting up and stay-bashing gang, but to the Chargehand supervising the repair and renewal of the copper fireboxes, who took me along to my new mate, Sam Maitland. Sam was well known throughout the workshops because, being an influential union man, a member of the Syndicate, he could be called in whenever a dispute was brewing. He was a small bald-headed character, but wiry and quite intelligent, obtaining some further vicarious prestige because his wife had recently been appointed a J.P. on the local Bench. Being such an ardent Labour man, a political view which I did not always share, we were to have some engaging discussions during our exertions inside the boilers where Sam, who had been in India during the Great War, also taught his willing pupil a few phrases of Hindustani and how to count up to 100 in that peculiar language!

Our immediate task was to knock out the drilled stays of the firebox casing, then start building up a new firebox from the existing crown which was left intact since it wasn't subject to so much wear. Then began an operation I soon grew to hate—scruffing!—chipping away the scale from the rounded corners of the casing with a pneumatic hammer, searching for cracks which the Boiler Inspector must confirm and arrange to have welded over. Then the crown nuts of the firebox must be carefully split without damaging the steel stays, the ends of which were re-threaded before securely screwing down new 1in. diameter nuts.

Now it was I appreciated Churchward's great advances in boiler design, that two feet of space between the firebox crown and the outer casing, the large radii at the corners of the firebox to reduce stress, the tapered firebox casing culminating 9in. above the long conical barrel obviating the need for a dome, and allowing for the engine to breast a gradient, or come to a sudden halt without leaving the firebox roof devoid of water.

Building up the new copper part-firebox was clean and more interesting work, and when it was assembled inside the casing all its intended stay holes were marked off with special long centre punches through the water way. When this was completed the firebox was removed in sections which were sent off to the drillers, work proceeding on another boiler until they came back for the final rebuilding of the firebox. After the complete boiler had been taken to the drilling jig, all holes tapped and steel and copper stays threaded in, the last operation was the insertion of the foundation ring, near-square in section and bent to the taper of the casing bottom, a somewhat tricky manoeuvre.

Brief though it sounds, this complete job would be spread over several weeks, and once again I was fortunate to be with a competent journeyman who understood his work thoroughly, was patient with his apprentice and keen that he should learn all he wanted.

"Keep striking while the molecules are disturbed!" he would tell me when we were inside the inverted boiler splitting the crown nuts prior to their removal. Sam was an intelligent, exceptional boilermaker, for most of his trade in the Bay were less refined, gruff, humourless and intense compared with the workers in the AE Shop; resolutely determined to get stuck into the job and knock up that Balance which, by Swindon standards, was always quite substantial.

Truth to tell, I was tolerating this work more bearably than expected when, after a couple of months, our Chargeman made a bee-line for me.

"We got no First Aid man on the night shift," he announced bluntly. "As you're the only qualified one in the Bay the Foreman wants you to be responsible."

As I have already mentioned I was pursuing the study with undiminished zeal, still maintaining word perfection as regards that little Black Book and applying its principles consistently in the regular practices with my four compatriots. By now our supremacy in Swindon was completely unchallenged with a report of our success appearing at appropriate times in the *Evening Advertiser*, that major trophy at Paddington luring us on but still eluding us. Three of our team worked in the A Shop and, myself now included, were regularly called upon to render aid though more frequently of a minor nature.

But in spite of my ever-keen interest in the subject I was most definitely unflattered by this bald statement and directive, objecting to the suggestion only to be told by the stern unflinching Chargeman I must take my turn on nights with all the rest. So there it was, a very dispiriting month for me though the 155 journeyman I was allotted to proved to be most pleasant and even light-hearted! Nevertheless night work seemed so contrary to human nature, working when you should be sleeping and sleeping—at least trying to—when most others were working. I remembered how quietly we had to move around the house as children when my father once did 'a month about' and the disruption it meant to the family routine; how he had gone off his food, having to eat at odd hours when the stomach often objected to it, just as mine did now.

During the midnight break after trying to eat my sandwiches I would wander outside into the keen fresh air and stillness of the night to gaze up at the wonders of the starry heavens, ponder what the future might have in store for me, and promise to make myself worthy of anything better that might come my way. It was the longest, dreariest month of my life in the Factory and when, at last, the end came and I sought a return on days for a spell, the Chargeman was aghast.

"Oh no! You've hardly started!" was his retort. "You're doing a good job there. We're hoping you'll stay on nights indefinitely!"

"No thank you!" I replied firmly. "You're trying to penalise me for my qualifications. If necessary I'll hand in my key and give up first aid altogether."

The tubby disgruntled Chargeman frowned heavily and walked away muttering he'd have to see what he could do; like me he was bearing in mind they were short of efficient First Aid men on the dayshift as well.

To my great relief I was not only put back on days but also paired with my former journeyman—I wondered if he had asked for me—and while in the course of time expected another hateful month, since most apprentices did that 'four weeks about' if not staying on permanent nights, found that I was retained on the day shift for the remainder of my time.

Five weeks before that ominous day, for there was no question of continuing employment in the Works as 'improver', the intermediate stage between the apprentice and fully-qualified journeyman, I approached Foreman Andrews about the possibility of spending at least my last month on electric welding which was looked upon as a special favour, and was ready to quote my night school record and Certificate if it seemed improbable.

It was readily conceded, so for a week I practised on any odd scraps of metal I could find, until the welder Chargehand deemed me safe to be let loose and start earning money for the gang.

I trundled the transformer around and plunged into each job so eagerly to gain all the experience possible behind the darkened protective shield and spluttering flashing electrodes, I'm sure I surprised him with my enthusiasm. Occasionally I would fumble at the essential arc and the white flux-covered electrode would stick to the metal instead of fusing, with the intense heat travelling back up rapidly unless the circuit was broken at once, but I'd seen it happen to the most experienced welders at different times and refused to let it embarrass me.

"I've been very pleased with you, and I only wish I could have kept you on," the Chargeman told me in parting on that last day. Whether he was sincere I preferred not to speculate.

I washed up and went off to collect my vital papers from the Managers' Office, the place where I'd begun nearly six and half years earlier. When I arrived I saw a few familiar faces already in the porter's ante-room, boilermakers who hadn't covered an apprenticeship even as much as I had, night school evaders who'd subsequently spent two years on alternate days and nights doing those monotonous and laborious things I'd managed to avoid.

One by one they were called in to collect their cards. I was last in and coldly presented by the elegant clerk with my credentials, the so-called indentures, which proved to be a very ordinary certificate.

As I emerged into the fresh air my contemporaries were stood in a little group perusing and comparing documents.

"Wot you got on yours then?" one asked me curiously, and the others became just as interested.

I read it out to them: "Freebury bears a good character, possesses good ability as a workman, and has conducted himself in a satisfactory manner."

"Aha!" they cried jubilantly. "We've all got the same!"
Satisfied at this, they went their different ways.

I studied my indenture again. It was true. No mention of any of those things I had hoped for; just the same rubber stamp given as a matter of course. Perhaps I had no grounds for complaint. Although I'd tried to give satisfaction throughout those years, I   157 couldn't forget I'd been forced by circumstances into something I never wanted, and my heart was not truly in my apprenticeship even during the happier days.

I suddenly felt so very uncertain and despondent, as if cast off among a pile of rejects in the very bloom of life—just entering manhood. The future loomed so bleak, even internationally. Neville Chamberlain had only just returned from Germany with his Munich Agreement, and Czechoslovakia was about to go the way of the other countries so blatantly annexed by Hitler. If one heeded what was written in the pages of *Mein Kampf*, surely war was only a matter of time, a possible holocaust with an outcome no one could foretell.

Yet once again I was resolved that when the ominous darkening clouds eventually rolled away I would never rest until that lack of security which had dogged our family over the years with its constant stress, vexations and forebodings was banished from my life once and for all.

Extracts from correspondence with Mr. K. J. Cook, O.B.E.,
Mechanical and Electrical Engineer of Swindon Works, and
author of Swindon Steam 1921–1951.

8th December 1977

Dear Mr. Cook,

I have read with intense interest your book: 'Swindon Steam'. No doubt you have received many letters in this vein from eminent contemporaries, but this might be one of the few from a lowly apprentice who "served his time Inside" during your term of office.

Your work might almost go down as a piece of Industrial History except, I feel, for one serious omission. In Chapter Seven, Austere Times, you state it was necessary to reduce expenditure in the locomotive works by £500,000. You cover very lucidly how this was handled by the management and technical staff, but I thought some mention of the hardship and deprivation it caused to the thousands of manual workers under your control would not be have been out of place, and might have completed an otherwise detailed account.

Before I entered the works as an office boy, I would hear from my father as he told my mother: "Afraid there's no balance for this week". Or: "There's a rumour we're going on three days soon." . . .

Then there were Black Fridays, when the austerity you mention really cut deep. For a fortnight or so rumour would be rife that a thousand or so had "to go" within a fortnight. The whole town would be stunned as if under a spell, hoping against hope it was just a rumour. But the axe would fall. Dad would come home and say: "Thank God we're all right this time." . . .

After I had filled my secret ambition of leaving top boy of my school, my father sought my chances of an apprenticeship. He was a 40/- a week machinist planing axle boxes in the AM Shop. All that was offered for me was boilermaking, the commonest trade of all and despised by most others.

Because my father was not a 42/- a week man, he could not even get me on his own type of work. Nevertheless I hoped things would change in due course, though I hated the thought of going in the Factory anyway; yet there was nothing else much better. So at 14½ I went as an office boy in the Platelayers' Shop, an office run by a solitary clerk, catering mostly for outstation work.

I enjoyed those 18 months. On my way to the Managers' Office I often passed the Running Shed and gazed in admiration at the beautiful shining monsters surrounding the turntable. Then, if not to the reception lobby with mail, perhaps past your door and up into the Accounts Office where the time sheets were worked out. . . .

At 16 I began my "Apprenticeship"—two years of doing nothing but rivet heating! I hated every day of it. I just knew I was worthy of something better. There was one consolation: I came under the AV Shop, but worked exclusively on the new work section of the AE. At 18, after considerable requests, I started out as a Plater on the new locomotives. I therefore saw the new horn-grinding machines and other innovations you mention installed in the AE shop.

I am sorry, but I had nothing but contempt for Mr.———— whom you mention. I regret to say that in my adolescent view he was a disgrace to the fraternity of foremen . . . Though one had to accept this kind of situation, I often wondered just how much the management knew of such goings-on. I was so tempted to write about all this to someone in authority, but to whom and to what effect? However, I kept up my Evening Classes at the College until I was 20 and I suppose this helped me to keep off boiler work until the last few months. At least I was grateful for that small mercy. . . .

You mention Mr. ———— as a "first class foreman". But I found it difficult to forgive him for the indignity he inflicted on my father only a few years before my Dad retired. The latter often told me he was the first man to plane axle boxes to micrometer limits, and as far as I knew he was the only machinist of experience not on his 42/-.

When the axle box gang, of which you speak, was formed my father had to be able to work the other odd machines as well as the latest 'planers'. Eventually he got his Union to speak for him yet again, but ———— insisted if he wanted his 42/- he should be capable of working any machine in the shop and set down the number of machines he was to be tried out on. I was back in the Works myself at that time; and I was disgusted. My father was respected by all who knew him, except apparently by ———— who, ignoring the blatant injustice of his case—someone who had given unstinting service to the Railway for nearly 40 years—subjected him even at that late stage to such an indignity for a paltry 2/- a week. Few other men on top rate could have measured up to this challenge, and Mr. ———— knew it. My father gave up after they tried him out on the third gang.

Why do I labour all these points? I am sure you are asking. Because I feel your book tends to give the impression that workers, foremen and management were all one happy family, and this was not so, you know. Most of the workers were proud of their Great Western engines, yes, but since the system had them at its mercy, they could tolerate it or else. . . .

To return once again to your book: I have enjoyed it so much it has stirred those memories I had thought were long forgotten. By the men on the floor you were well respected. The message soon got around

"Look out! Cookie's about!" when you were on your numerous jaunts to the A shop. Your quiet unassuming manner comes through in the book, I feel, and that "Trip" incident you mention in the railways sidings I really enjoyed. Only someone who had participated in that annual exodus could fully appreciate the incident, the panic, then your alert and efficient handling of the situation.

All this makes me feel there is a real need for a work showing the other side of the picture to that of the excellent account you give from the managerial angle; namely, the plight and conditions under which the ordinary man laboured. It might be considered a corollary to your work, but only someone who has experienced this at first hand could do it justice. A modern Alfred Williams effort, if you like! You have planted within me the seed for such a work, which might be fictional based on solid fact, or largely autobiographical. But it must wait until I have completed a present assignment.

. . . I moved here with my family in 1957, anxious to get back to the sea. Around about it is a delightful corner of England you must visit one day if you have not already done so. I have a pleasant modest little home which suits our needs. Mr. Gillespie has visited here, and if I may make so bold, if you were ever in the vicinity I should feel honoured by your presence.

My sincere apologies if I have bored you.

Yours truly,
Hugh Freebury

Dec. 29th 1977

Dear Freebury,

Thank you very much for your letter dated 8th December. I am very pleased to learn of your progress and congratulate you on having overcome and risen so well.

I would not for a moment dispute the facts and distress as set out by you—there is no doubt that there was great distress from time to time, and, of course, much as we regretted it, there were undoubtedly abuses and incorrect decisions by subordinates and no doubt sometimes my name was mud although I endeavoured to keep things impersonal. I do not however accept your story about ————.

I think one must accept the position as set out by you, realising that this did not apply only to Swindon, but was sweeping the country, either then or very shortly after.

I think it is necessary to keep a balanced picture of things over a period of time. In my opinion, the workers at Swindon were, in general, fairly contented, partly evidenced by the fact that at any opportunity they returned to the Works and, of course, I worked amongst them for a considerable period.

The flow of apprentices and semi-skilled through the Works could be looked upon as a supply of cheap labour but the main railway workshops were great training grounds at a time when such facilities were not available elsewhere on the scale they now are and many of them have done well with the facilities for study also available.

I fear, although a long way before my time, that Alfred Williams was a complete misfit and one finds such from time to time.

I wish you a very Happy and Prosperous New Year 1978.

Yours sincerely,

K. J. Cook

16th January 1978

Dear Mr. Cook,

I was delighted to hear from you, and to know you are obviously still active. If it means anything at all, I assure you your name never was mud, in my view, amongst the manual workers. You and the other managerial Staff were certainly treated with great awe, even by the foremen. Indeed, the flurryings when it was known you were on your way often amused me, because if one is doing his job efficiently and conscientiously there is nothing to fear from a visit of the Archangel himself!

However, you held the respect of the very ordinary men for your quiet unassuming manner, and behind that somewhat severe exterior one sometimes felt was a basically understanding person. . . .

I would not want you to think I am embittered. As you say, the conditions and attitude existing in the Works were common throughout industry; and looking in retrospect at my own life I see it all now as a definite pattern. It is like looking at the rear of a tapestry for so many struggling arduous years, then suddenly being able to see the finished picture on the other side. . . .

Your point about the sacked men returning to the Works at the first opportunity is true, of course, and used to irritate the older employees. One reason was that the system in the works was not an exacting one in general, if not very well paid; but another was possibly the insularity resulting from a one-industry town in itself creating a closely-knit community, which factors tended to stifle ambition among the ordinary workers.

May I conclude (at long last) by reciprocating your kind wishes for 1978, and indeed many subsequent years. How wonderful it must be to look upon a life so very full as yours and the splendid contribution you have made to our railways and therefore our country, and no doubt outlived so many of your contemporaries in that field.

I sense you still have an active mind; this together with good health and a sense of humour are blessings from the Almighty beyond all price. It is my sincere wish that there are many more years of pleasant reflections, if not active participation in life ahead—perhaps even another venture in the literary field! It is a marvellous means of self-expression which, as in the case of your book and myself, can give so much pleasure to others.

My offer to show you around this little corner of England—the birthplace of British History you know—still stands, if you have not yet been round this way.

Yours sincerely,
Hugh Freebury

January 23rd 1978

Dear Freebury,

Thank you very much for your further letter, and your "History of Mathematics" which I find very interesting. You must have done an enormous amount of research into the subject.

I am not likely to write any more books but Ian Allan did write and say they would be very pleased to publish another one from me, and someone had suggested a subject to them. I felt, however, that it would fall between two stools—not technical enough for engineers and too technical for ordinary locomotive enthusiasts. I have not been to Didcot but have spoken to three of the branches of the G.W. Society. The maintenance work which they are undertaking is quite amazing.

Thank you for your kind invitation to call on you if in your district. I have been round there several years ago but I do not generally get that way now. However, I am making a note of your address.

Yours sincerely,
Kenneth J. Cook

Lastly: Endorsement in a personal copy of Swindon Steam 1921–1951.

To Hugh Freebury,

Who had active connections with the Locomotive Works and served "Swindon Steam" in the years 1933 to 1938, and who has written to me very kindly concerning the contents of my book.

I am happy that he has found it interesting and that it has brought back memories to him.

I was delighted to hear of, and congratulate him on, his progress and prowess.

Kenneth J. Cook.

23.1.78   163

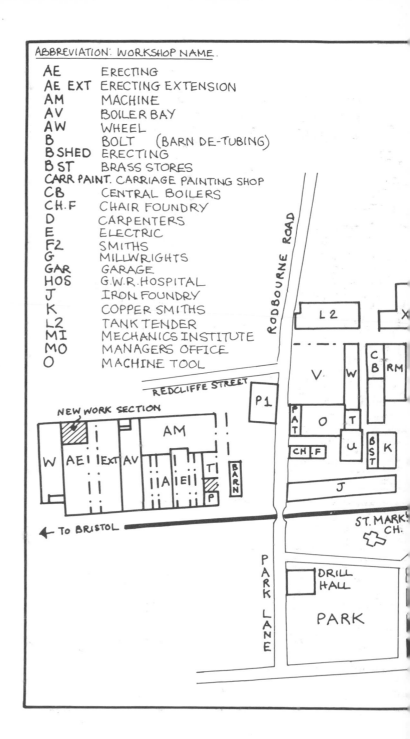

ABBREVIATION: WORKSHOP NAME.

Abbreviation	Workshop Name
AE	ERECTING
AE EXT	ERECTING EXTENSION
AM	MACHINE
AV	BOILER BAY
AW	WHEEL
B	BOLT (BARN DE-TUBING)
B SHED	ERECTING
B ST	BRASS STORES
CARR PAINT.	CARRIAGE PAINTING SHOP
CB	CENTRAL BOILERS
CH.F	CHAIR FOUNDRY
D	CARPENTERS
E	ELECTRIC
F2	SMITHS
G	MILLWRIGHTS
GAR	GARAGE
HOS	G.W.R.HOSPITAL
J	IRON FOUNDRY
K	COPPER SMITHS
L2	TANK TENDER
MI	MECHANICS INSTITUTE
MO	MANAGERS OFFICE
O	MACHINE TOOL

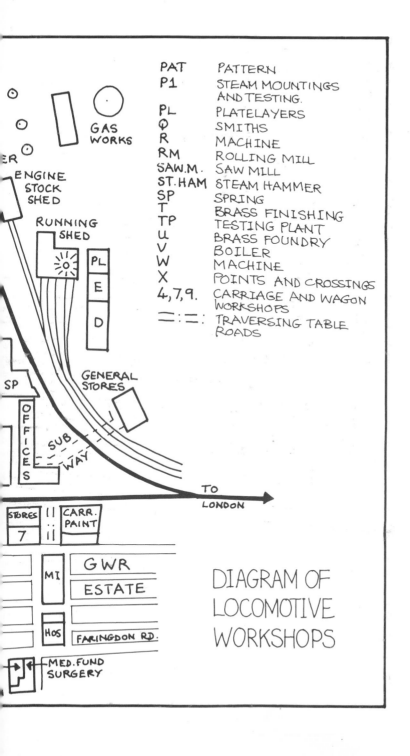

PAT — PATTERN
P1 — STEAM MOUNTINGS AND TESTING.
PL — PLATELAYERS
Q — SMITHS
R — MACHINE
RM — ROLLING MILL
SAW.M. — SAW MILL
ST.HAM — STEAM HAMMER
SP — SPRING
T — BRASS FINISHING
TP — TESTING PLANT
U — BRASS FOUNDRY
V — BOILER
W — MACHINE
X — POINTS AND CROSSINGS
4,7,9. — CARRIAGE AND WAGON WORKSHOPS
═:═: — TRAVERSING TABLE ROADS

GAS WORKS

ENGINE STOCK SHED

RUNNING SHED

PL

E

D

GENERAL STORES

SP

OFFICES

SUB WAY

TO LONDON

STORES

7

CARR. PAINT

MI

GWR ESTATE

HOS

FARINGDON RD.

MED.FUND SURGERY

DIAGRAM OF LOCOMOTIVE WORKSHOPS